NOWHERE BUT DOWN

FROM TRAGEDY TO TRIUMPH. ONE WOMAN'S TELL ALL - ABOUT THE SECRET TO LIFE'S SUMMIT

ADELLE ROSALIA STEWART

Enjoy the climb!
Adelle.

Published by Peak Publishing
ISBN Paperback: 978-1-7774255-0-0
Book Design: Stoke Publishing
Cover Photo: Lindsey Egan

CONTENTS

PREFACE

I have been writing this book for over 10 years. Although I had no words on paper, I knew it would be written - I just didn't know when or how. It wasn't until 2020 "happened" to me that I realized the story had been waiting for this year, before the final chapter of this phase in my life would be completed.

Once I started writing, I couldn't stop. The rough draft of this memoir was completed in 75 days, and my story was ready to be heard. I had many revelations as I wrote, for writing has always been a therapy for me. Many days it doesn't feel that "I" wrote this book, but I feel it was downloaded through me, from spirit above, from the depths of my soul. As the words appeared on the screen, I read them, seemingly for the first time, from my human perspective and gained a clear under-standing of what happened to me and why.

This book may not be an easy read for everyone. This is a trigger warning for death, sexual assault, domestic abuse, and critical illness. The goal in sharing my story is to be hopeful and to help others. As it turns out, a by-product of writing this story to help others is that I was able to heal myself.

1

MEAN GIRLS

I wasn't always a good person.

In my 20s, I was a terrible friend. Not that I was trying to be a bad friend; I just thought other people needed to have the same thoughts and opinions as I did in order for us to get along.

You can call me the black sheep. I've always lived on the outer edge of whatever is considered normal. As a woman, I was never the domestic type. Until I got cancer, I didn't know what a carb was and didn't care. I cooked to survive (hello pizzas and perogies); I didn't bake - there's Costco for that (I'm not even a snobby pastry eater, I only care that it comes in bulk). And laundry? Well, blacks, colors, towels, and under-wear, it all cleans the same together in my opinion, if you avoid buying whites.

I also have never wanted children of my own. I know I know, even the most un-domestic goddess typically has the undying maternal desire to procreate. Not I. Never did, never have. It was just an intrinsic knowing inside me, or maybe better said a not-knowing. While I was growing up, the thought of having kids never crossed my mind. I learned I was an outcast on this matter at age 15. I had spent the past two summers babysitting and raking in cash, hating the job (kids) all the way through, which I just thought was a normal feeling. It was normal for me.

I remember a conversation one evening over dinner. Our family was discussing some other child's misbehavior when my brother Tyler piped up, "I'd never let my kids get away with that." The comment made me take pause, and I asked him, "How do you even know you'll have kids?" He replied, "I dunno. I just do." Huh. My whole life, the concept had never been an inkling in my mind. So me being the opinionated loud-mouth I was at that age, I shared, "Well, I am not having kids!"

Let me tell you. I wish I had kept that a secret. From here on in, I endured 15 years of comments such as "You'll change your mind," and "Oh, that's just a phase." And for the first 10 of them, I would vehemently fight back and snap, "NO, I WON'T," until I gave up and pacified the maternal beings of the world... "Yes, sure, I might." New topic, please.

I am glad we are getting to a place in the world where we are putting a stop to asking this question of women. Plus, I'm almost 40 now so people are beginning to realize I was serious about the decision. I am a fantastic fur-mom and that's enough for me.

Back to the story of how not wanting kids made me a bad friend. Before I knew how to navigate relationships where our opinions weren't all one in the same, I thought no one should have kids. I began aggressively trying to convince my friends they should want the same child-free life as me. I'd say to my friends who were getting married right out of high school. "Ewwww, you want to have kids? How gross. Changing diapers, staying up all night, and don't even get me started on being pregnant. I can't believe you're going to have kids. Are you crazy?!"

I projected my inner insecurities and anger of other people pushing kids on me by pushing not having kids on them. I wasn't enlightened enough back then to realize what I was doing, and I see now how poor of a friend I was for it.

I have difficulty hiding my true emotions. When I was younger, I didn't know how to be there for my friends in the ways they needed. I didn't know how to be there authentically for things that I didn't give a shit about personally. I didn't understand how to insert healthy boundaries in order to maintain relationships with friends. So when they started getting married and asking me to be in their bridal parties, I said yes. And then when we would go to the flower shop for fourteen hours looking at centerpieces, I'd be the one staring out the window and offering to go get a round of coffee. I wasn't trying to be mean, but I didn't know how to be supportive participating in something I didn't care one ounce about. I thought feigning interest on behalf of the bride would mean I was going against my own character and admitting that I was "wrong." I was happy with my un-domestic ways. But what I know now versus then is how to be a friend that cares about my friends, regardless of what they care about - and do it authentically.

I just had to get kicked out of a bridal party first to get me started on that journey.

Have you ever been kicked out of a bridal party? That's an ego punch. I even begged to get back into it even though I didn't want to be there in the first place. Looking back, I'm glad she said no. There wasn't enough time for me to change, and I wouldn't have been a better bridesmaid. Six months later, when one of our other friends got married, I was a better bridesmaid. I wasn't 100% authentic – a person can't grow that fast – but fake it 'til you make it is a simple strategy for starting to drive improvement in your life. What I did get was a glimmer of what it felt like to be a good friend. It was enough to get me on my way towards personal growth, become an authentic friend while being true to myself, and have healthy boundaries.

The next time I was asked to be in a bridal party – I declined. My friend respected that decision, and we maintained a friendship through it. Some may read this and think, *ADELLE! How dare you not suck it up and be a bridesmaid.* But you see – the world and mainly women – don't have many healthy boundaries. I can love and support you, come to the bridal shower, be authentically there for you and join in your glee – from a distance. But I cannot buy the dress, wear the heels, do the hair, the nails, the matching jewellery, the flowers, the squeals. I can't pull that off for an entire year of wedding planning. I know that, so I don't. My friends know that, so they don't ask, and we all get along swimmingly.

The story doesn't end there. I was more of a lousy friend and had more bad friends. In my teens and early twenties, the main issue was I didn't have control of my ego. At all. I was a fire-breathing, opinionated dragon. And when I wasn't opinionated or backed in a corner, I was afraid and, as a result, would compensate with foolish pride.

Another story that sticks out in my memory is when a friend and I planned an epic road trip through the Canadian Rockies between the Christmas and New Year's break – completing the loop on New Year's Eve at a big city bar. We both drove sexy little sports cars at the time, and since we were road tripping through the Canadian Rockies during winter, my dad wanted us to be a lot safer than we would be in our cars, so he lent us his 4x4 tricked out Cadillac Escalade. Its window tag would have been worth over $120K, and for a young little 22-year-old to head off down the road in that, I was proud.

Pride. Ah. Another sneaky little ego-based feeling. I know it now, I'll admit it; I talked way too much about that damn truck. I felt like a rock star using the valet at the hotels; I pumped the base and referenced how cool the truck was to my passenger probably 600 times too many. Guilty as charged.

But we were both young, and we both didn't have total control over our communication or regulation of our emotions. Instead of having an authentic conversation with me, my gal pal gossiped about me to our friends back home via text. When she started being on her phone more than talking to me, when we started bickering and being snarky with each other, I knew something was up. But we were in a different city, far from home, and it was supposed to be the best New Year's Eve of our lives. We were supposed to take the town by storm. We had new dresses and heels, and we were supposed to go and have the night of our lives, post our highlight reel on Facebook and be epic.

Instead, I snooped on her phone while she was in the shower. I'm usually not like that and can honestly only count two times in my entire life that I've done it. Once, on this night, and the second when I had an inkling that my husband was cheating on me. So in my defense, I have only done it in instances with very good reason.

So. There we were, in our swanky hotel room, with my friend in the shower. Her phone was on the night table, and I scrolled and scrolled, succumbing to gut punch after gut punch, going back on days of gossip about me. I remember holding the phone, shaking, looking around the room at my suitcase, still packed. I looked at my keys. I was ready to leave. Leave her there, in the shower, eight hours from home. It took all my willpower not to go. Instead, I put on a smile, and we had a terribly shitty night out on the town because of my horrid ability to hide my true emotions.

But frankly, looking back, I am grateful for these experiences. They provided the foundation for such inspirational personal growth. I surely wouldn't be the person I am today without those lessons, even though I lost each and every one of those friends over them.

I've actually never had the same type of friendships after that either. We were a group of about six girls who were all BFF close. But as we got older, it got harder to have us all together. What would end up happening is straight out of a *Real Housewives of Beverly Hills* episode: the one who wasn't there was the one who got talked about. As the group gatherings continue, and the gossip about the missing woman escalates, you start to piece together what might be happening the night you have a date night instead of a girls' night. Long story short – we imploded.

Since then, I have multiple best friends in my life, but we are not all friends. I am friends with each of those best friends, but we never all come together. Looking at it now, maybe it's a form of protection for me. Perhaps I still have work to do. Maybe writing this book will be cheaper than going back to therapy after all.

2

A LOVE STORY

My first love died the summer I was 22.

We met one May Long weekend. Now I don't know where you're from, but May Long Weekend in the Canadian Prairies is the official kick-off to summer, even though there's a 97% chance it will be snowing.

Since the beginning of high school, my friends and I had been packing up and heading to the lake for May Long. This year was different, though; this year we weren't going to my friend's dad's cabin to be partially supervised. We were 18, graduating high school in a month, and packed up our cars and trucks with tents and coolers before heading off to spend a weekend in the bush to see if we could survive on our own.

High school was a weird time for me. I wasn't popular, but I wasn't a loser. I was somewhere in between and could hang out in any part of the high school where each of these groups resided. I was just happy being in the middle. High school is so weird, isn't it? Certain kids hang out in certain places, where other kids instinctively know they are not welcome. I guess it's not all that different from modern adulthood. I wasn't "naturally popular" like some of the other girls, and I didn't care to be wildly famous and make them accept me, which was both a skill and a tactic others chose to master in order to be accepted. I could have gone that route, but I didn't have the energy. So I floated. Black sheep, even then. They were grouped into middle of the high school stairs (mid-popular), left side of the stairs (popular), and front of the school mezzanine by the fountain (least popular). I never had to resort to hanging in the library, but I can say that I was kind to every person who did.

I barely dated, and my first boyfriend didn't even go to our school. Again, always living on the perimeter of whatever everyday life is "supposed" to be. So needless to say, I was single and ready to mingle this weekend at the lake. I wasn't overly cocky about it, and truthfully, I was quite shy. I hid behind pounds of wild makeup and lacked a lot of confidence. I don't remember being told I was pretty and beautiful growing up, at least not in the way I wanted to be pretty. I had long, wildly curly hair that the adults around me loved, so I hated. I longed to be like the girls with their poker straight locks, so when people (grandma) would say how beautiful my hair was, I resented it. Needless to say, I didn't consider myself a hot ticket.

When we got to the lake, suddenly my BFF and I were the talks of the town, or the lake I guess. She was 6 feet tall, rail-thin with spiky blonde hair. I was short and petite with a long lion's mane – we made quite the pair. We ended up setting up camp close to this new group of exciting boys who were also from our hometown, even though we were three hours away from the city—what luck. One of my gal pals overheard one of the boys say he was going to marry me. BLUSH! But he seemed a little wild and crazy, and I had my eye on this quieter, sporty, frosted tip spiky-haired hottie named Graham. Luckily, he had his eye on me too.

We all partied and got to know each other, having a blast, full of hugs and laughs, learning that topping the neck of your beer with lemon rum was the only way to consume alcohol on the long weekend. Then we went home.

Wait, what? Yeah, true story, nothing actually happened between us that weekend. But upon returning home, I couldn't stop thinking about Graham. Later the next week, we were cruising the main strip on a Friday night (that's what you did on weekends in my town... drive upppp and downnn the same road, heavily utilizing the U-turn lane, subwoofers in your trunk, and your heater for those spring nights where you wanted to wear a cute tank top but it was freezing out. The only way to drive around was with the windows down, and the heat cranked. #heatersandtanktops would have been our hashtag (if there were hashtags back then).

On one lap – we passed them! The crazy boy who wanted to marry me was driving with Graham. I don't remember how I got his phone number (social media wasn't yet a thing), but I did, and while driving my 5-speed Turbo Sprint down the strip, navigating shifting and traffic, I also called him on my cell phone and asked him to be my date to our end of high school celebrations called graduation.

He said yes! I had now gone from the high school black sheep, single most of my life, to the girl who asks the boy she barely knows to come to the most important day and memory of a teenager's life!

It was, indeed, all meant to be. We were official from that moment until almost four years later. People all around us loved us as a couple. We were each other's firsts; we spent entire days cuddling in bed in his parent's basement, walked our dogs, had supper with our families, travelled to Mexico, switched from cruising in cars to cruising on his motorcycle. We also partied, and partied hard. We were the king and queen of the bar. I was his trophy girlfriend, and he was one of the kindest, best looking, funniest people that, to this day, 20 years later, I have ever met.

Then, he started to pull away.

He started partying a little bit harder, hanging out more with his badass friend, who was heavily into recreational drugs and way too much drinking. He went to raves and parties out of town that I had no interest in. He started ghosting me and not returning my calls on evenings we had plans to be together.

I was young, full of jealousy and rage, and actually resorted to stalking him one night he was avoiding me. I called his parents, asked when he left and who he left with, then drove downtown and tracked down his green and purple motorcycle at one of the local bars, where we had it out on the sidewalk. But nothing changed.

His behavior continued on and on until I snapped. My mom's best friend, who we grew up calling our aunt, died from cancer. She had been in palliative care for a while. We knew it was coming, but she was far too wonderful of a lady and far too young to die of this disease. I called Graham in tears, expecting that he would drop what he was doing to spend the day with me and help me grieve. He didn't. He was not prepared even to consider changing his plans, and that was that.

That was that. I don't remember the conversation that officially ended the relationship, but knowing me back then, I can only assume that it wasn't a pretty one.

Years later, his mom told me that he had done these things - the ditching, the ghosting, and the avoiding - on purpose so I would be the one to break up with him. He didn't think we weren't right for each other for forever, so he discussed it with his mom and started treating me poorly, so I would be the one who broke it off. He had told her that it was the only way because if he had broken up with me, it would have broken my heart. Screw him was my initial reaction. Now, though, I know he had been right.

Because I hated him after I broke up with him, I was able to move on. Life changed rapidly from here on in. My "aunt" Cheryl had left my mom some money out of her will. Her only rule on spending it was that it "not be for anything remotely practical." No stocks, no bonds, no renovations, no debt, nothing but something fun.

Cheryl had always been quite the woman. Single most of her life, she had a beautiful little home, was fiercely independent, a world traveller, career woman, and tough as fucking nails. She also never had kids of her own, so she basically was my idol. It made total Cheryl sense that she'd put that kind of stipulation on an inheritance.

Mom and I had been taking horseback riding lessons for the last few years; as a little girl, I always dreamed of having my own horse. I had spent my youth going to summer riding camp and winter lessons when I could, pitching in so my family could afford it. Horses had been in my blood since I was a toddler. Books of horses, rides at the fair, pushing my dad away at three years old, riding my first horse telling him I could do it "by myself!" If you have a love for horses, you know it's just something you are born with. My mom had been the same way. She had a horse when she was younger – but as many mothers do – she had given it up when she got married to raise a family.

It only made sense that, with the funds from Cheryl, we buy a horse.

Getting my first horse quickly distracted me from the loss of my first real love. But as time passed, my hate towards Graham softened. By this time, my family had gone a few steps further into horse ownership, and my mom kept the horse we had originally bought to share, and I got my very own horse. We also picked up and packed up the only home I had ever known and moved out to an acreage to have the horses on our own property.

During these massive distractions and realizing there's more to life, Graham and I started talking again. I would ask him to look after my Pomeranian, Boo, on weekends when I was going away with girlfriends or my family. I had gotten Boo while Graham and I dated, so he was his "dad" and loved that dog as much as I did. There was no one I trusted with him more.

We met a few times, and I remember the first time was down by the riverbank. We were able to talk it out, rationally and reasonably. I had been able to see through my pain and temper my inner dragon so I wouldn't overreact. It was the start of something between us, but I didn't know what. I didn't even know what I wanted it to be.

He had an epic summer trip planned to the interior of British Columbia with his best friend and his cousins who lived there. Graham and I had made a trip out there ourselves one summer, and it to this day was one of the most incredible places I've gone. We went to a party in the mountains, swam in Okanogan, watched the local rodeo, and drank in a garage where his cousins jammed with their band. The interior of BC is one of my favorite places on earth, and I got to visit it with the person I loved and his extended family, who I also absolutely adore.

I was excited for him to go back and spend more time there. I was also jealous but mostly happy. We met up again the day before he left. I remember the meeting vividly. It was at a pita restaurant next to the parking lot of the office where I worked. We chatted, reminisced about our trip to BC, and as the conversation rounded, there was an unspoken feeling, a silent agreement, that when he got back, we might just try things again. The song "Fast Cars and Freedom" by Rascal Flatts came on, and I can barely explain the dynamic between us. We had never had a song, but forever since, we didn't have to say it to know this one would be it.

He hadn't been gone more than a few days when one night I was lying in bed, and our phone rang in the wee hours of the morning. We had this weird phone that "talked" who was calling, and you could program the names in yourself. In my half-sleep, after the first ring in my sleeping stupor, I heard "Adelle, it's Gaham" - the recorded tag my dad had made for Graham's family's number.

What? No. Graham was in BC. It's like two o'clock in the morning. It must have been "rat boy on his cell phone," which was my dad's tag for my younger brother. He must be breaking curfew - again. As I talked myself down, suddenly, I heard my mother's feet padding down the stairs and a knock at my door.

"Adelle – it's Marie. Pick up the phone."

"Hello?"

Graham's mom's voice filled the line. "Adelle, I'm so sorry... he's gone. Graham – he's gone."

Just days after arriving in BC, Graham died in a single-vehicle motorcycle accident, and we, to this day, still don't know why or how it happened. I've visited the site, and while it is a gently winding mountain town road, the curve was perfectly visible. He had not been drinking. For all the partying we did, Graham was poker straight on riding sober. There had been no other traffic; a car of strangers and then his best friend were first on the scene after it happened. Had it been an animal? Did he not navigate the road appropriately? There were no brake marks, nothing to indicate what had happened; all we knew was that he was gone.

3

CHASING GHOSTS

I had heard a story while Graham and I were still happy in our relationship. A family friend's daughter had lost her boyfriend in a tragic accident. The daughter went on to fall in love with and marry his best friend. When I heard the story, I immediately had the thought, "That is going to happen to me." At the time, I wrote this off because I was dating Graham and we would be together forever. It was also my first brush with tapping into my intuition, and I didn't even know what intuition was at that point. I thought that I simply romanticized the notion of a sweet love story born out of tragedy. I often thought about it and had this inkling it was going to happen to me. And then it did.

Graham's death rocked our community. The church was full at his funeral. From baseball to competitive hockey, neighbourhood pals to high school buddies, everyone and their families loved Graham. He was good. Sure, we partied too hard and drank too much and tested the limits of growing up, but we were good kids, at the root of it all, and Graham was one of the best. Because he was so respected, he sure did have some good friends. I'm not sure why out of them all I chose the worst one out of the group.

It was natural for us to dislike each other: the childhood best friend and the serious girlfriend. I was taking his friend away from him, and he would steal time away from us. It was a classic story about a boy's first true love.

Kent and I did more than butt heads about our custody of Graham's time. I also had a deep dislike for the badass he brought out in Graham, and true to form, I wasn't skilled about hiding it. Kent was an oil patch rigger, the stereotypical kind: strippers, blow, and weeks away from home at a time. When he'd come back to town, he'd have more money than he knew what to do with, and it was time for boys' nights and boys' weekends, no girls allowed. I'm all for spending time apart, but at the core of my values, I've always had this thing against doing drugs. I lost a good friendship over it before, and I didn't like being with friends who did them or around my boyfriend doing them. Call me controlling, whatever. So when Kent would come to town, tensions were high.

It all changed after Graham died. His friends took me under their wing at the funeral, including Kent. I remember talking on the phone to his two good friends, pleading with them not to forget me. I had lost a piece of myself, and at only 22 years old, it was not something that was clearly defined. It was a lost and wandering piece of me that knew Graham and I hadn't been together, but after our last conversation, I felt we weren't apart, and the blackness of the uncertainty was vast and unsettling.

After the funeral, his friends and I continued to connect. Graham had been our only real connection in the past, and now his memory was our lifeline to each other. Kent and I seemed to bond the closest; we had lost the most. Time went on and we grew closer, our grief soothed by each other's company. He was still drinking and partying too much, but I stopped noticing. I started appreciating hanging on his coattails. Everyone looked forward to when Kent was back in town. He was the life of the party, the funds of the party, and when I was on his arm, I received part of those accolades too. We fell messily in love.

At the same time we were grieving, we were growing up. We were in our early 20s, and it was time to move on with our lives. As we still lived with our parents, the next practical step towards adulthood would be to move out. Growing up, my parents instilled in me a strong fiscal responsibility, so it made no sense to me to waste money on rent. Instead, I had lived with them longer than I may have wanted, but I socked money away, month over month, to save up for a down payment on my first house. Since I was now seriously dating Kent, it only made sense that we move in with each other. Except by this time, he had solidified the habit of spending everything he earned, so the investment came solely from me. Ever the wise, my parents ensured we were both protected and had us write and sign cohabitation agreements.

It was all peace and love at first, and perfect for me that he was away for two weeks at a time. I would have two solid weeks of focusing on my horse. I had started coaching lessons at the stable I grew up learning how to ride at, and then when Kent was home, we would have fun and party, and just as my tolerance for him began to wane, he'd go back to work again.

Dating Kent worked as a negative coping strategy until I realized it had been a Band-Aid for my grief. I did not do the work on healing from Graham's loss. That uncertain and wandering piece of me that I had lost in the vastness of his death was still floating around in the abyss. All the things that I was unsure about in our relationship began to compound with the uncertainty I had towards Kent, and I took it out on him. I became very possessive and jealous, repeatedly calling night after night, sometimes until one o'clock in the morning, to see if he was out partying and doing hookers and blow while he was away at work. It kept me up at night and surely pissed him off as he ignored call after call. The house of cards we had built the foundation of our relationship on was beginning to waver under the weight of our mutual grief.

His drinking got worse, the drugs more abundant, and our fighting intensified. We were so young, so naïve. I don't even remember what we would fight about, and I genuinely don't remember what we fought about the night it ended. All I know is that we screamed and yelled; he slammed the door and left; and I called my dad crying, screaming "What am I going to do?"

Stuff and things, they chain us down. Material possessions drive our decisions, decisions to stay or to go, and the "loss" of it all if we left. What we need to be asking ourselves is, what does it cost us to stay. This was a lesson I know now that I didn't realize then, and one I had to learn a few more times in my journey for it to stick.

Our cohabitation agreement was what saved us because, despite our hate for each other, the terms of our separation were clearly defined. Since I paid the down payment, I got to keep the house. We had gained about 25% equity in the home since we bought it, and I owed him half of that. And when I say me, I mean my dad because I would have been homeless without his help to keep me in the property. I don't think my parents wanted me back home as much as I didn't want to be there. It was a rather unremarkable separation after that blowout, and I was happy to end up coming out on top when I sold the house a year later, when the original price of my home had doubled.

Our relationship was over, and I didn't grieve it long. I have always felt more comfortable being single, and it was time to let my hair down again. I moved into a brand-new townhouse that was a short 10-minute drive to the stable, started riding more than ever, coaching more lessons, and bought a new horse I planned to compete in rodeos with.

The horse I had bought was a bit of a knot head and had a shady past. We affectionally called her Hell Bitch, and she was not ready to rodeo. So that first year, she stayed at home while I went out on the road to learn the ropes with my friends. By learning the ropes, I mean drinking too much, partying too hard, dancing with cowboy strangers, weekend after weekend. We became quite the talk of the town, this little travelling rig. A group of younger guys travelled together and called themselves the wolf pack, so we called ourselves the cat pack. The truck was full of five or six of us each weekend; half of us were a few years older than the others, so we affectionately called ourselves the cougars and the cubs. I have seen the inside of almost every bar in the small-town prairies, but don't ask me where exactly we were because I don't remember.

I had turned 25 that spring and felt like it was a year to live it on up: quarter century celebrations, all year long. To this day it is still one of the most fun summers I've ever had. We took way too many photos, outlining each rodeo's inner workings, and by Monday, fellow rodeo competitors would eagerly await the documentation of the shenanigans had by all posted on social media. To give you an idea of just how ridiculous we were, here's a short summation of some of the photo album titles:

"WTF That's My Broom," "Who Broke the Bed," "How to Get A Cab 101," and "PS: You Only Have Three Tires On Your Trailer."

I honestly... can't even. As we continued down the rodeo trail, we all met the wrong boys, and I fell in lust with an Australian saddle bronc rider. Predictably, as the summer went on and he prepared to go back to his homeland, I became a stage-five clinger; he broke my heart; and I got a tattoo in Sanskrit that said, "Believe" to get me through being dumped so brutally.

I can't wait to be an aunt so I can tell my nieces and nephews all these "in my day" stories.

As fall came to a close, good things must end as they always do. My Australian love did indeed leave, and I was most definitely a blocked number on his phone- with good reason. The Cat Pack headed back to our civilian lives, already dreaming of the next rodeo season to come. What we didn't see coming was the fact that none of our lives would ever be the same.

4

MEETING MR. WRONG

The writing was on the wall. The proof was in the pudding. The signs were flashing danger.

I have always been a little defiant in the face of anyone telling me I shouldn't do something.

So I did it anyway.

Mr. Wrong wasn't someone I met in the street, or at the bar. I guess it's 2020, so I should keep up with the times… Mr. Wrong wasn't someone I met online; he was someone that a one-time good friend of mine had already broken up with.

Yep. I am that girl. I broke the unwritten chicks before rule. In actuality, we weren't friends anymore after that New Year's Eve disaster from a few chapters ago, but I'm sure sorry for it now! Needless to say, Mr. Wrong had been an asshole back when my ex-friend was with him. Drinking too much, fighting too hard, and he kissed another girl in the bar one time as well. Or "she kissed him" was his plea for her mercy and forgiveness. There was also a time when she called me, crying in a panic, thinking he would hit her. If I recall correctly, he had thrown a broom at her and shoved her up against the wall. I pulled up to her house, threw the car door open as she ran from her home and into the car, where we made a mad getaway.

Funny how your brain blocks things out when it comes to love. I didn't remember the kissing of the girl in the bar, the broom throwing, the best friend rescue getaway – until I sat down to write this chapter.

When Mark and I reconnected, I did remember that he drank too much, but it was also about five years later when our paths crossed again. I made a mistake in assuming that because she had since done something so hurtful to me, maybe she had been wrong about him. She talked behind my back and couldn't address the real issue she had with me, so I though perhaps, just maybe, she had exaggerated about him. I only ever got her side of the story back then, and he seemed like such a gentleman now. Plus – people can change; I do believe that. I don't think many of them do, but we can – if you want to!

He was a perfect gentleman for the first few weeks. He picked me up in his fancy truck, took me out for delicious suppers, and pulled out my chair. He brought me flowers, cute gifts and treats just because he saw them and thought about me. Then he moved on to buying me diamonds, and I kept getting wooed by his generosity.

When he was with her, they had wanted, planned, and were excited to have a big family. Six kids to be exact. As we continued courting, he knew from years passed that I didn't want kids. As we kept dating and I enjoyed being spoiled, this lingering issue of children was not lost on me, nor in the conversations about our relationship. I would bring it up frequently, and he would always abate my fears. He was wooed by me, loved me, and said that he'd rather have me in his life with no kids, than have a child with someone he'd love half as much.

I believed him.

At my core, it felt yucky, uncomfortable, out of alignment. I ignored those warnings and I ignored my intuition that was screaming at me to walk away.

I dreaded telling my parents about him... They knew the "old Mark" from our high school days and, rightfully so, thought he was still that person. But I was always that person who thrived on defiance just to make a point. I remember the day I told them. I recall vividly where we were and the look in my mom's eyes. He had not even come with me to supper, I told them alone. They were more supportive than they probably should have been. And, with time, his undeniable wit and charm won them over too.

I loved his family, and they adored me. I must admit that many parents always have. Breakups have always been hard for me because even when I don't love the person I'm with anymore, I don't want to lose the family that I have gained. His mom was the perfect farm wife. They lived on a little acreage, and Mark and his dad worked together, owning their own business in construction. Maggie, his mom, was incredible. She worked full time at the local grocery store, and then with all her other time, she was either cooking, cleaning, gardening, canning, or being the most amazing domestic wife in all the land. I still, to this day, don't know how she kept up with it all. They had at least three full-size deep freezers because she worked at the grocery store and she only ever bought things on sale. So she would stock up on dollar days and could stretch a grocery penny seven ways from centre.

She always had everything. She doted and catered to her family more than anyone I have met. I don't like the taste of red meat, so I stopped eating it when I was about 14. His sister was also a vegetarian for a time. We would each get our own meals every time we gathered. If they were having burgers, she would make chicken fingers for me. Her dinner table was full, every meal, of the main course plus salads, cheese and pickle trays, water, lemonade, cola, at least three dressings, and any condiment you could imagine.

Don't get me wrong – my mom – can cook. She can cook and bake up a storm. She makes tiny chicken statues out of deviled eggs; they have peppercorn eyes, a carrot nose, the works. But growing up, she didn't cater to dietary preferences. You ate what was on the table or bust. That was fine. But you can see how, when Maggie came into my life, I felt absolutely spoiled. At first, I was shy and embarrassed. Mark had advised her of my eating preferences before I even met them, so the first time we went over there for supper as a couple, she had special chicken for me because they were having steak.

Mark's dad also loved me. I was a farm girl, unafraid to do, learn, or try anything. He gave me my first real backhoe operating lesson and left me to my own devices after about 15 minutes of instruction to call his son and tell him he found a good one. They even hired me a few times on projects with tight timelines and were short on labour. I loved it.

His sister, who carried the torch of hating all of her brother's girlfriends, more than tolerated me. I started going to her to get my nails done. We visited, and I was so proud when she would tell me she actually liked me.

His family became my family and living just ten minutes down the highway from them, we spent a lot of time at their farm.

Things can change obviously, and they did, but these are the memories I choose to fill my thoughts with, not the resulting aberration they became in years to come.

5

KEEPING UP WITH THE JONESES

As things got more serious, I had more reservations. By this point in my life, I had become quite the runner in dating and relationships. Runaway bride, runway girlfriend, call it what you want, but when things get tough, I would channel my inner Julia Roberts as Maggie Carpenter, and leave. But this time, my friend tribe was a small triangle of three great gal pals. We did so much together when it was just the three of us, mostly all revolving around horses. Bikini barrel races, rodeo road trips, calling on cowboys, gosh, we had a good time. We were young, and we were living it up.

But now, we had each met more serious boys, all at the same time. It all transpired and came to fruition during a trip we took to Palm Springs. Like a pact. We were the cat pack, after all. We were down in SoCal having a blast; we were present with each other, yet each was sneaking a text here or there to the boy back home. It was November, just after that epic summer of rodeos and partying was coming to an end. It was becoming apparent that our lives were unlikely ever to be the same again. In short, we were growing up. At the time, it seemed like the natural progression. Grow up, get married, watch your friends have babies, be the coolest pseudo-aunty ever. Plus, who wants to be the fifth wheel while your two best friends get on with their life without you?

So even though I wasn't feeling the vibe with Mark, I kept dating him. He kept buying me diamonds. I'm pretty sure I had a tennis bracelet, a necklace, and a set of earrings by this time. I don't even like diamonds. But I fooled myself into thinking it was all going like it should. The six of us, three couples, would hang out together, have fun – mind you not the same kind of fun we used to, but more grown-up fun, I guess. We were all reasonably serious; I still had my doubts, but maybe this was just a part of growing up, I told myself.

The problem started to arise when our relationship began moving faster than the others. Like, way more quickly. It had only been five months before Mark and I had begun looking at acreages to buy and move in together. At the time, he had been living with his parents on their property after a broken engagement a few years prior. He was ready to spread his wings and had found someone else who wanted to share the country lifestyle.

To this day, I have no idea what my parents were thinking about all of this. I had just got out of my last bad common-law relationship with Kent two years ago. I don't know whether they were saying things and I was ignoring them, or if they weren't saying them at all. But they supportively came to all the properties we looked at, thank God for that. I can't imagine the place we may have ended up at if they hadn't been there. Location, location, location has always been their first three rules for buying real estate. We looked at land to build on just a mile down from his parents; we looked at a 100-year-old character house that had been completely redone on the main floor with a commercial kitchen (like I needed that to warm up pizza and cook perogies, but it looked cool). It had a three-season porch, a front porch, secret servant stairs, and three stories with electric heat and no air conditioning in the middle of the Canadian prairie. Thank God both our families were there to talk us out of that purchase or I'm sure had we been left to our own devices, we would have ended up there, 30 miles out of town, on a very niche property to try to resell after we got divorced.

We ended up putting in an offer on a great place only 11 miles out of town on 40 acres with a more modern house and tons of room for horses. As unsure as I was about our relationship, buying this property locked me in. I was living in a townhouse in the city at the time and calling the cops on my neighbours on the regular for their after-bar parties, hating my city life. My money was tied up in that property in the city, but Mark assured me all was well when he stroked the cheque for the down payment. He really did love me. Ha.

So there I was, half-delighted, half-certainly-unsure about what I was doing. But my friend Heidi and our other friend were all still in relationships - so like, what else would I do. Plus, they rallied in support of Mark too. So good-looking, well-off, funny as all hell, I began to think the problem was me, so I kept hanging in there and keeping my gut feelings at bay.

We would have a few months to wait for possession of the farm. It was still early spring, and we wouldn't assume ownership until the end of summer. I felt like I still had time to feel this all out and fall in love with him. Instead, shit hit the fan when he proposed the day our offer got accepted - just six months after we had been dating. I knew something was brewing when I was coaching a riding lesson, and he texted that he was on his way there. He never came to the barn. Nervously I sped up my process of putting my horse up; all my fellow coaches and friends were hanging about giddily. I turned my mare out to pasture as he pulled up. Suddenly everyone vacated the tack room, and as they did, the power went out, so we were in the pitch dark. If that wasn't a sign of sure doom, I don't know what is. He asked me to marry him. I remember being grateful it was dark so that he couldn't see the terror on my face.

Everyone was waiting just outside the barn; I could hear their excited chatter. We would walk out of that barn, and everyone would know and would cheer. What do I do? We were going to live on my dream property. How many 26-year-old's have their own farm? My horses, the land, these thoughts were all racing through my head. Everyone was waiting. He was waiting. It was still dark.

When someone asks you to marry them, especially in public, HOW do you say no?! What pressure. I could probably do it now, but back then, I was too young, too naive, too uncertain about who I was to stand up for what I wanted. The smoke and mirrors of material possessions and a good life, the alternative of being single at 26 and not having anyone to hang out with... there were so many people around outside, waiting to cheer. The ring was incredible. He had said he would give up kids for me. He just bought us an acreage. At that moment, I convinced myself I was the crazy one.

So I said yes.

We exited the stable, and everyone, of course, cheered. We got in the gator and did a victory lap around the outdoor arena. And by we, I mean my friends and I. We left Mark in the dust. Looking back, I can see how much this "status" of marriage can have a chain hold on young women. We are just starting to celebrate women and independence, and view it in a different light, but just over a decade ago, being married was an important achievement and status symbol.

I didn't see it then. But the instant I put that ring on, I became his possession. Things started to change, and I realized later that by buying me things, he figured he owned me. It was sneaky, and for many years I didn't see it, and even when I started to wonder - the thought didn't cross my mind to do something about it.

As soon as we got engaged, the things I thought he had loved about me he wanted me to change. He was suddenly insanely jealous of everything. With my free spirit and cowgirl attitude, he no longer wanted me to travel to barrel races. Our first big row was when he didn't want me to go to the Calgary Stampede with my friend Kendra. This trip had been planned since before Mark and I were even dating. Kendra and I had gone to the Stampede years before, danced, watched rodeo and chuckwagon racing, and had a grand time. This year, we had tickets to the Kenny Chesney concert. Mark was suddenly all over me about cheating, hanging around cowboys, projecting his insecurities on to me. I was 26 years old and can proudly say then, and now, that I have never, ever, stepped outside of a relationship. The thought never even crossed my mind, because instead, I historically ran away from the entire relationship before I even got that close! I had never given him a breath of an idea to mistrust me. But here he was, literally demanding, that I not go.

We already had $100 tickets, purchased the fall before, and he wanted me to let my friend down because he was on some weird jealousy rampage? We fought, and we fought – and don't get me wrong, I loved to argue. But he wore me down. Wore me down after seven months of dating but hadn't broke me yet. I stuck hard and fast that I was going to the concert but conceded to only going for one night instead of three. I ruined Kendra's weekend, our girls' weekend, because my jealous fiancé couldn't be happy that I had a life outside of his.

My second instance that the universe was telling me to get the hell out of that relationship was later that summer - the night before I was supposed to leave with Heidi for our provincial barrel racing finals. His dog was sick, and he thought I should stay home. That's a pretty big stretch of an excuse, but we fought about it until 2 in the morning. I finally called Heidi weeping and said I wasn't going. I was ruining the weekend for both of us since we were planning to take my moms trailer, and we had already packed it up the day before.

I cannot even recall the conversation with her, but she somehow talked me down by telling me to get a few hours of sleep and we would make the decision by 7 am, and she would respect whatever choice I made.

Well, I woke up, enough of the "real me" that I defiantly decided I was going. Let me tell you, if you have to be defiant that early in a relationship – get out, it won't get better. It was my first time competing in the finals. I had turned Hell Bitch into a respectable barrel horse, and we had worked hard. Mark should have been happy for me. Barrel racing is basically an all-female sport, so I was technically going to hang out with 300 girls all weekend. So I woke up, called Heidi, and we went. This time at least, I stayed all the nights. My mare and I made it to the short go for the final day, and we played out the weekend on my schedule.

As the fall went on, when times were good, they were great. We got possession of our farm and moved in together. Amalgamating and intertwining our lives, I thought I would never live on a superior acreage than what we had bought. When he was in a good mood, we had the most fun ever. He could always, always make me laugh; he was one of the funniest people I've ever met. We would sing and dance together around the house, unpacking boxes and using brooms as stand-up microphones; it was genuine fun. While we were moving in, we decided to be responsible adults and get the furniture and the carpets cleaned, so Mark hired someone he knew to do this.

He went off to work one day, and the cleaner came in. I was home unpacking and cleaning. I don't recall how it came about, but Mark suddenly was accusing me of cheating on him with the carpet cleaner a few days later.

What.

This accusation was so out of left field, but he was sure of it. At first, I remember being dumbfounded, then mad and fighting back, calling the cleaner on the phone right then and there. He didn't answer, and I left him a message that he needed to call Mark back and tell him we didn't sleep together. We kept fighting, and wow, he already had a knack for wearing me down by now if you can't tell. He got me to the point where he was leaving, and I was weeping, standing desperately on the running board of his truck, holding on to the side mirror, begging him not to go as he continued to drive down the driveway, speeding up until I let go and fell off.

Just writing this, thinking of the Adelle I became, makes me want to take her in my arms and rock her.

The trouble with gaslighting in relationships is you don't see it coming, especially when you think you're in love, and when there are "good times" sprinkled in between. These three significant events that occurred in the span of three months time should have warned me off far and wide. But we had the farm, and I had the ring. How could I ever give those things up? I didn't see it as mind control and narcissism then, but I do now. Combined with still being young and attracted to shiny things, I couldn't imagine handing over my one karat diamond ring and loading my horses up off that farm.

So I stayed, and we got married.

6

SETTLING DOWN - OR JUST, SETTLING

I didn't know it was abuse.

I didn't think it was.

Some days, I still think it is too harsh a word to use in my situation.

I grew up in the days where the definition of abuse would illicit the idea of Garth Brooks' music video of *The Thunder Rolls*. I never had a black eye, was never thrown into the wall.

I had a dream about him the night before writing this chapter. I had not planned on writing about this part of my life until later in the process, but I woke up in an anxious panic and knew it needed to come out. That's the thing about healing – once you set the intention you are going to do it, you don't always get to choose when the time is right to let it go. I had dreamed about him; I dreamed I was still with him. The feelings in that dream were as real as the days I experienced them. I think those are the times I know that it was real, and it was abuse: emotional abuse, narcissistic, gaslighting. And not calling it out as such would be a disservice to any woman or man going through the same thing.

It is wrong, and you don't deserve it.

I could tell you to get out as soon as you recognize it, but I know it's more complicated than that. First, you have to acknowledge it. Then you have to have the guts to do something about it.

I didn't.

Our wedding was nondescript. We had 162 guests, and the whole shebang cost only five thousand dollars. I don't know if I downplayed the wedding planning because I didn't want to get married or because I'm such a tomboy. I do think it was more of the latter, but I also wasn't excited about planning the wedding either, more likely due to the former.

We had no wedding cake, no bridal party, no speeches. We had no first dance, no wedding favours. We said our vows and I couldn't even look him in the eye. I brushed it off as nerves.

We went home that night, and life went on.

I was so excited to be living on the same land as my horses; I spent many beautiful hours with them every day. We began boarding horses, and Mark moved his family horse to the property so we could ride together. But riding together quickly turned from a quality time date night into an argument. Suddenly, Mark had a bee in his bonnet about the horses coming first before him. I rolled this around in my head and came up with the conclusion that if it came down to him having a late supper because the 4-legged wild creatures penned between 4 fences who rely on being fed by a human to survive counts as them coming first – then yep, they do. Make yourself a sandwich.

I had already quit competing. The rodeo horse I bought before we met was now going for trail rides. Going to rodeos now that we were married was "out of the question." So instead, she sat around, getting sassy and unused, until I sold her after she bucked me off three times because she didn't want to go slow anymore and I was holding her back.

But it was okay, I told myself. There was lots to do around the farm. My rodeo dreams were over, and I had other young horses to raise and train that needed my attention anyway.

Things changed slowly. I didn't recognize it, and I genuinely don't even know if narcissists and abusers realize what they are. Mark was very particular. Maybe it was his mom's particularness that rubbed off on him; I don't know. But I remember the little things that started to add up to be big things. Like – the laundry.

Yep, the laundry.

Our bedroom was at one end of our bungalow, and the laundry machines were directly under our bedroom, but the stairs were at the opposite end of the house. So I was perfectly content to take the pile of dirty clothes and huck them down the stairs. There were only the two of us living there, and we rarely, if ever, used the basement. To me – this was fine because the next time I went downstairs for something out of the deep freeze or when I had run out of socks, I would scoop up the pile and throw a load in.

This method was, inconceivably, unacceptable to Mark. So much that he would lose his ever-loving temper any time I did as much. I was SO LAZY.

We did our own laundry. He did his and I did mine. He couldn't fathom the thought that I would throw towels in with my T-shirts and refused to have his cottons treated with such disrespect. There were sparks of the stubborn old me, things he must have intrinsically knew were a lost cause on his mission of control. Making him do his own laundry was one area I stood my guard.

I could go on and on with other minute household idiosyncrasies like dishes, hair in the sink, pet hair on the couch, and other daily dealings that would have him diving off the deep end, but I think you get the point.

I still didn't see it as mistreatment. I thought this just must be marriage and tried to counsel us through it. I hung a sign on the fridge that said, "You have to love the whole person – not just the parts that are easy to like." My philosophy on relationships was different. I felt that you have to wake up and choose each day. Choose to remember why you love that person in the first place and know that the small things that are important to YOU may not be important to THEM, so you lovingly accept that and move on with your day, knowing that there are things that are important to THEM that you could give a flying eff over. He didn't see it that way. If it wasn't important to him, it wasn't important, and if it was important to me, I was wrong.

I still did not see this as control and manipulation even when I began experiencing a burst of anxiety hearing his diesel truck come down the gravel road. After work, I would be relaxing on the couch, hear his big jacked up rumbling truck and immediately jump off the couch – actually, I wouldn't jump. We had a huge picture window in the living room that the driveway led up to. I would roll off the couch and army-crawl around the corner and then jump up. I would check the stairs to make sure I had taken the laundry all the way and began to busy myself, tidying the kitchen or the bathroom to avoid another argument, being yelled at, or being called useless and lazy. As time went on, the instances that would set him off became more sensitive, especially when he started drinking heavily. Yelling became drawer slamming, became keychain throwing. I needed to do better to avoid this.

I still had some sense of myself and a tiny sense of safety. When we went out, we began taking two vehicles everywhere. Mark's drinking was becoming out of control, and he regularly drove under the influence. He refused to let me drive if I was with him because he was "fine," so I started taking my own vehicle.

One night in the middle of January, he called me with his last sense of self and cellphone battery, saying, "I ran out of fuel. Come get me."

"Come get you where?" Silence.

He had been on a snowmobile rally that day. It was -30, and the wind was howling about 35 miles per hour. I had no idea where he was; I just knew the rally's last point where he should have been coming home from.

I got in my truck and started driving down the road with my hazards on, the wind driving snow across the highway, causing it to pile up on the shoulder. I drove about 20 miles when I saw a slightly bigger snow pile. It was Mark's sled, on the side of the highway, and he was passed out on the other side of it, shivering, trying to get out of the wind.

Still – not a problem that I had the guts to do anything about.

His behaviour continued to escalate. He worked even harder to exert control over me, and the drinking got worse and worse. I was living on eggshells. He began to yell at me about having kids and starting a family. Uh, what? We decided that long ago. Nope, he had changed his mind. And now that his narcissistic, controlling personality had the edge over me, it was time to push me – right over the ledge to the thing he had lied about not wanting all along.

I almost, almost did it. I was at the point where I was so utterly broken and would have gone against everything I had ever wanted to comply with his demands.

Until he started to lose his patience with me dragging my feet about getting pregnant, and he began making mistakes.

Like cheating on me.

The fighting was on the daily now. No one knew. No. One. Knew. It happened behind closed doors. I wasn't walking out of the house with a black eye, just a bruised heart. No one knew because I barely knew.

I came home one day from work, and to my surprise, he was already there. He finished all he could do at the new construction home he had been working on for his friends. They had started as customers, became Mark's friends, then, as the job went on, more and more of their relationship began to decay. Mark was thinking of quitting.

He was telling me all this, and I went into the bathroom. On the counter was my hairbrush – *weird*, I thought, and *NOT GOOD! Hairbrushes do not belong on the counter, and I don't want Mark to yell at me!* As I grabbed it, I noticed a hair extension in the bristles.

A hair extension? I thought to myself as I held it up to my own hair. Much longer and the wrong color. And, I didn't have hair extensions.

"What's this?" I asked him.

"Your hair," he said.

"No this is fake hair, not my hair."

"I don't know; it's nothing. You are probably imagining it."

Me, in the frail and unconfident state I am in, tugged at the hair extension, doublechecked my scalp to see if maybe I had a large pore in my head it came out of and said, "I don't think so."

Then – he started to get mad. Shit, I went too far.

I dropped the subject, threw it in the garbage, and went out to feed the horses.

When I returned to the house, he must have checked the garbage and had enough of an ego check to understand this looked bad on him. So he explained that Tanis, the customer's wife, had come over and begged him not to quit the job. But that was all. Why not just tell me that then? Because he hadn't even remembered it; it was so inconsequential. She used the bathroom before she left, and she must have used your brush.

I thought silently to myself, *And she didn't notice that she left a long giant extension in my brush, on the counter, after opening our bathroom drawers to get it out in the first place?*

The more I questioned, the more pissed off he became. But I was mad too. I asked if her husband Don knew she had come over, and asked if I called him, would he know. Then, Mark royally lost his shit. Looking back is how I know this was manipulation and abuse because a gaslighter will escalate a bad situation to a worse one when you begin to gain the upper hand. He instilled fear in me to get the outcome he wanted, the outcome he needed. He retaliated, screaming, "YEAH, FUCKING CALL DON! FUCKING CALL HIM, DO YOU WANT ME TO CALL HIM?" and threw his phone across the room and slammed his glass full of rye down.

"No, no, no, honey, I believe you."

And for a time, I did.

I had to.

I even forgot about the hair extension (filed it away and locked it up) until more strange behaviour began. Mark became very possessive over his phone. I trusted him completely and never, ever, had looked at his phone. I didn't care to. Honestly, genuinely, the thought never crossed my mind.

But he kept acting weirder. And less mean. And whereas in the past three years I never had an inkling to look at his phone, he began to have a problem with leaving it out in the open anywhere. When that began to change, I began to change. For weeks, months, I noticed him becoming very secretive. Where he used to just put the phone down on the footstool with the screen left on to fade, he would click it dark. If it buzzed when it wasn't in his hand, he would jump to reach for it. And god forbid, forgetting it anywhere near me would make him literally get up and make an excuse to take it away from my vicinity. This behavior continued; I never said anything. I silently observed and wondered. It went on and on, never waning in his possessiveness of that little black box.

Until one day, he forgot.

This all happened back in the day that preceded apple and android phones, and phones didn't even have passwords. So all I had to do was roll the little white ball, and it came to life in my hands. Message from Brenda. Who was Brenda? Maybe a customer. Click.

Full frontal breast shot.

Must be spam.

Scroll.

Brenda: "What are you doing?"

Mark: "Sitting out back in the backhoe watching the pit fire burn."

Mark: "Send me a pic."

Brenda: "The kids are at home."

Mark: "Please."

He asked for it. It was not spam. What was going on?

My heart was racing; he was just 25 feet away on the porch, getting dressed to go outside. I grabbed my cell phone and snapped photos of the screen and forwarded them to my friend Laura.

Suddenly I heard his boots stomping across the landing, "I forgot my...."

As he walks in, he sees me with his phone in my hand, trembling.

And I walked out.

7

STAYING OUT OF SHAME

I was leaving.

But he didn't make it easy.

He texted me that he'd kill himself if I left.

But the infidelity had been the icing on the cake for me, and it broke me. It needed to break me. I applaud any other man or woman who can leave a toxic relationship without a big "event." Often times, there are a lot of reasons, compounding ones - but we still never go. I should never have married him, and I should never have stayed for as long as I did. I am so grateful he cheated, so I had the strength I needed to get up, dust myself off, scrape the cobwebs out of my eyes, and realize what a mess I had got myself into.

The hardest thing I had to do now was call my dad. It was time for someone to know what was going on, and I had to ask for help.

It was early one morning; I can't remember if I was going to work or if the drinking had started early and I left to escape. But I was driving in my truck when I called, and when my dad picked up, all I could choke out was that I needed a lawyer.

My family never questioned my decision to go, and I'm sure they knew all along that our marriage had been a bad call. So we lawyered up and began the process.

Mark didn't want to get divorced, and he didn't want me to leave. At first, he was willing to do whatever he needed to get me back (classic gaslighter). I asked him to move out, and he did, for a few days. He wanted to talk about moving forward together during these days, and I wanted to know what happened. When, where, with who and how many times.

Every time I asked him to start a conversation, we could only talk about what he wanted to talk about and refused to tell me anything about the other women. I knew there had been two, one more than once, and that extension in the hairbrush had been a clear sign I had chose to ignore.

At the time when I found it, I knew. I knew. But you know what stopped me from just leaving based on a theory and my own unhappiness? Shame. Shame that I had failed in a marriage after being a wife for only two years. Shame that I'd have to admit my highlight reel on social was a sham. Shame that I couldn't be a good enough woman for him to love only me. Shame that I might have to move back to the city and off the farm and give up my dreams.

Leaving without an "event" would have been hard, no doubt. And looking back, I needed to live these harsh lessons to learn, but I implore you, you can learn from other's mistakes instead of living through them yourself. So leave. Go if you aren't happy and run if you are being mistreated. It will be challenging but staying could kill you.

His mom tried to get involved. I would be lying on the couch in a depressive bliss and ignore her calls. I knew why she was calling. She had been cheated on, too, but she stayed. She had been cheated on worse than me, with her husband impregnating her own sister. It made for interesting family Christmases, but I did admire her ability to forgive and forget. I knew I'd forgive Mark, but I'd never forget, and I'd never trust him again.

I contemplated staying; I really did. But I knew in staying I would be living a life that wasn't true to me. I wasn't the jealous type anymore. I had got over worrying and wondering if my partner was cheating on me, and I didn't want to go back there. I knew I would never trust Mark again, and I didn't want to go back to being the girl who would call repeatedly through the night and live in wonder and worry. I knew that is what I would do if I stayed. I had come too far in my personal journey to turn back now. So I dug in and held my ground with the divorce.

Taking my power back pissed Mark off, so he upped his narcissistic game. He moved back into our home. Against my wishes, he moved back into the house and into the spare room, and we began living legally separated, together. I don't know if he thought he could wear me down with this, it sure as hell pushed my limits. But here's the thing about an abuser - they just keep trying and trying to regain control, any way they can.

One night I was lying in bed, and Mark came into the room, our master bedroom. He walked past my side of the bed to his, flipped the covers, and got in.

"What. Are you doing?" I asked him.

"I'm fucking sleeping in my own bed; that spare room is shit."

"No, you're not. We are getting a divorce; get out."

"You never have sex with me anyway. It's just sleeping, and you've got your pillow fortress around you. I couldn't touch you even if I wanted to. Get over it."

So I got out.

He effectively wormed his way back into a position of power when it became clear to him I was slipping through his grasp. And at this point, a gaslighter will do anything to shake the foundation you are trying to build for yourself to keep up the guts to leave. But I'd had enough. So I got up, took my dog, and moved to the cold and uncomfortable spare bedroom.

You would think it would stop there; how much more control could he get?

But every day that went on, he kept upping the ante, drinking more, partying harder, staying out later. When he came home in the wee hours of the morning, drunk as a skunk, he would have to pass the door to the spare bedroom where I was sleeping to get to the master. My heart would beat in fear every night when I heard his truck rumble up. What kind of mood was he in? Would he pass by my room and go pass out or would this be a night he wanted to yell at me? It was a 50/50 chance each time, and many mornings throughout that fall, I went to work having been up half the night, defending why I wasn't going to work it out with him anymore.

Things could get heated those nights. I would be lying if I said I wasn't terrified living there, but I didn't know how to actually leave. We had agreed to cohabitate in our matrimonial home, legally separated until our divorce details were final. My dog was there, my cats were there, my horses were there, my customer's horses were there, and I had a lot of responsibility to the animals every day. Plus – I wanted to be the one who stayed. Our lawyer said to stand guard and don't leave the marital home if that was my goal. So, I stayed and prayed.

It got to the point where I feared things were going to get physical. I was exhausted from the arguing, which was only getting worse and worse. If you're in a narcissistic relationship and need to get out, you need to be ready to deal with this. Reach out, lean on your friends and family. I didn't. I was too ashamed that this was happening to me - that this was the person I had married – so I kept it all a secret. I knew there was no way my parents would let me stay there if they knew this was how I was spending my nights, trembling in fear for my safety, but I couldn't leave my responsibilities, and I wouldn't leave my horses.

So, I did all I could to keep myself safe, and at first, I started sleeping with a rifle under my bed. This wasn't anything new to me, as throughout our marriage, I was afraid of sleeping alone out on the farm in the middle of nowhere. When Mark would stay out all hours of the night, we had a running pact that became a joke – that he better phone me before he was coming home, so I would know the rumblings on the porch in the middle of the night was him and not an intruder and wouldn't shoot him. For all the control he had over me, he must have known I was serious about this because, for the most part, even in a drunken blackout state, he would call so that I wouldn't shoot.

It came to the point where having the guns in the house at all, even under my bed, began to leave me fearful. So, stupidly, instead of moving out - I took his guns. At this time, I didn't even have my Possession and Acquisition License, which is a requirement in Canada to own or be in possession of a firearm, but I took his grandpa's shotgun and his dad's rifle and hid them at my parent's. I can't even remember what excuse I made up to my parents that this was somehow okay, that I was so afraid for my safety that I had to remove weapons from the house, but it was okay that I still stayed.

This was a bizarre time, this phase of knee-knocking terror and anxiety being in my own home, yet I was finding my voice, building myself, finding myself, starting over. I began to become defiant to him in a very non-confrontational way. He was still possessive over me, and he liked that I stayed at home in fear like a meek little mouse. So when I started telling my friends and family that my marriage was over, the support I received was overwhelming. People weren't judging me- they were supporting me! It fueled my internal will to take my power back, but psychologically I knew I couldn't turn that fast on Mark. So, as a 29-year-old adult woman, I began sneaking out of my own house to save face from my soon to be ex-husband.

I would leave the house with my Pomeranian Boo in yoga pants (me, not the dog – he was much too fluffy for spandex) and tell Mark I was going to Laura's. Not exactly something he would be worried about. What he didn't know was that my miniskirt was in my purse, and under my hoodie was a cute little tank. I started to go out, go to concerts. Laura's was my home away from home, and wherever I went, Boo went, so it was his second home too. He would hang there while we went to town and danced to country music, and the pieces of me that had withered began to bloom.

My sneaking around was all going fine until Mark began to gain a clue that he was losing ground yet again. Then, he realized his guns were missing.

8

CODE PURPLE

It was an early January morning, and if you're not familiar with January in Saskatchewan, Canada, it's cold. Like, Alaska cold. I was in the bathroom getting ready to go to work, and Mark had once again upped his game as he felt the grasp of his power slipping away. Now he wasn't just drinking every day until all hours of the morning; he was drinking in the morning. I heard the familiar crack of a long neck, and my only thought was, *Thank God it's a beer and not rye.*

He padded past the bathroom while slugging a sip, just waiting for me to take the bait and say something about it so we could fight. But I didn't. He continued to search for something that would set me off, and unfortunately, he found it.

"Where, the FUCK, are my guns."

After weeks of them being gone, safely stowed off the property, he had realized they were missing. I didn't know how bad this was going to get, but it didn't feel good. Nothing other than angels at this point guided me to close the doors to the bathroom and lock them. We had a classic 1960's home with only one bathroom on each floor that had been renovated with a more "open" concept. So our bathroom was huge, with a corner jacuzzi, separate stand-up shower, and a huge double sink counter in a big u-shape and the bathroom had two doors. One door was close to the master bedroom for an en-suite entrance, and the other door served as the main bath entrance.

I got the main door, which I was closest to, locked quietly and swiftly. I then had to run around the corner and slide the other pocket door shut and lock it from the master bedroom entrance. I did it just as he was walking down the long hallway from our walk-in closet towards me, and when he heard the click of the lock, he lost it.

I don't know why I had the inkling to lock the doors; again, no explanation other than angels above.

"Unlock the FUCKING doors."

Why did he want in? I didn't have the guns.

"NO," I said.

"Where are they."

"They aren't here."

"WHERE ARE THEY!"

"I took them to my dad's."

From this point, my memory of the conversation goes blank. I was no longer in control of my mind and body. I can only recant what happened, not how it happened.

I felt I was in danger. When I refused to unlock the doors, Mark continued to escalate. What was I going to do? I was locked in the bathroom that didn't have a window that opened. My only decision was made for me, as I instinctively backed away from the pocket door, just as he punched a hole in it. From there on, I was riding on angels wings.

I ran around the corner and out the other door, which gave me a two-second lead time on Mark. Boo was lying directly in my path, so I scooped him up off the floor. My purse was somehow perfectly placed on a kitchen chair in my path that I could looped an elbow through while running through the kitchen, onto the porch, down the stairs, and out to the garage. I turned over my poor diesel truck in -45, gave it no opportunity to ignite the glow plugs, let alone warm-up, barely made it out of the garage without taking half the door off with me, and sped away.

I hope no one ever has to experience that feeling, and if you are currently living it, please know there are ways to get out.

I arrived at my parent's home in nothing but my pyjamas and slippers. I had almost become a victim of physical violence, and for the first time in my life, I felt what it was like to have nothing and everything all at the same time. I was safe, and I had Boo. But I had left my two cats, three horses, and five boarding horses back there, all of whom needed my care. How was I supposed to navigate this? There was no way. I couldn't go back.

That day I officially moved in with my parents, and over the coming days and weeks, they made room for my dog, my cats, my horses. I returned to my bedroom in the basement, having gone from a California king to a single mattress in one sleep. My customers had to find new homes for their animals in the middle of winter. It was a gut-wrenching feeling.

Back at the house, seemingly unperturbed by my escape, Mark made a call and sicked his dad on us. His dad showed up at my parent's house that morning, demanding the guns be returned. I couldn't believe he wanted Mark to have them back. On more than one occasion during our separation, I had called his parents to intervene when he would text me that he was at the bar and would kill himself if I left him. How do you decipher gaslighting behaviour from mental illness? Mark got his temper from his dad, so our discussion about who was keeping the guns escalated quickly, to the point of the RCMP being called in.

Here is where the law and common sense collide. Neither my dad nor I had our possession and acquisition licenses, but my father-in-law quickly whipped his out. The officer turned to me with regret in his eyes and informed me we were not legally allowed to keep the guns, even though I feared for my life if they were returned to their owner.

"I'm sorry, ma'am, that's the law."

"He's suicidal!" I blurted out. "Not only am I afraid he's going to kill me – he's been threatening to kill himself if I leave him. And you're going to return his guns to him?"

At this point, rationality began to return, and when the officer asked my father-in-law about this, it was a fact that he couldn't deny. They had made more than one trip to the town bar to pick him up after I sent them screenshots of his threats of self-harm. The officer released control of the rifles to him and then headed back to our farm to complete a suicide risk assessment on Mark.

Two things happen when you call 911 for someone who is suicidal. The person either willingly goes with them or is arrested and then goes. Mark agreed to go willingly, and I took that opportunity to go back to the farm, pack as many suitcases as I could find, grab my cats, and leave everything else behind. He was assessed and released and home by nightfall, but his dad agreed to keep the rifles at his home.

To date, that had been the lowest, most humiliating, embarrassing, devastating point in my life. Just weeks ago, I had been married, and to the outside world, living the dream. A hilarious husband, a DINK life-style (double income, no kids), horses, building a blossoming equine facility... Now I was living in my parent's basement out of a suitcase, and I felt like I had lost everything.

I stopped communicating with Mark, and it was for my own mental health. Whenever my phone would ring or alert me to a text, my heart would begin to race, and I'd start to sweat. I'd avoid looking at the screen but when I finally did a wave of relief would cross over me if it wasn't his name on my phone. We could not have a conversation without screaming, so my dad became the mediator. This worked for a few conversations, until again, that gaslighter realized he was losing control of the fire.

He demanded to talk to me and stonewalled my dad from any further conversation. How the hell was I going to get rid of him now? So I picked up the phone the next time he called. He wanted to meet. I never wanted to see him again. I felt like one of those girls in a movie who had been kidnapped, and to get her captor to release her, she had to play into his game. So I agreed to meet him.

We met one winter day in January at a coffee shop. I had only agreed to meet him in a highly public place. If he wanted to lose his shit there, at least I'd have witnesses. He did not understand the divorce proceedings. He didn't realize what equity was. I was trying to navigate my separation and be his counsel, explaining that half the equity was not half the home's value. He had been agreeable to let me stay and buy him out when he thought he would be getting a $250,000 payout from our half-million-dollar property. Uh, not quite. When he realized that he would receive half of what we had paid down on the house, which wasn't much really after only two years living there, he now refused to let me be the one to stay.

I went to many a counselling session over this. I didn't want to leave, and I didn't want to let him win. I didn't want to release this property I had dreamed about and finally got - a property I thought I would never be able to replace. My counsellor did a visualization with me. She asked me to imagine the turmoil, the arguments, the drawn-out legal proceedings, the fatigue, the hard feelings, the finances, and then asked me to imagine that after all that – it was mine. She asked me to take a visual tour around the property and tell her how I felt.

I felt... empty, sad, and angry. In my visualization, I walked around the farm, and I looked at the outdoor arena Mark fought me about building because it was too big and dug up too much land. I looked at the hayshed we built with our wedding gift money and how he held it over my head during every argument that he got nothing out of the wedding, despite the building being his idea. I remembered when my horse Littlebit got into the hayshed and stuck between bales all day, and how when I called Mark for help, he refused and told me to figure it out. I looked at the shelter we built, that was built his way, on his time, how he made me feel like a slave. We worked until he said we were done working, no matter how tired I was. I ran and fetched tools and shouldered being called an idiot when I didn't know what a crescent wrench was and brought the wrong thing. I remembered the arguments we had, the cupboards slamming, and I saw the hole in the bathroom door.

I decided to let that dream go.

Mark and I sat at the coffee shop that day and wrote our settlement agreement on a napkin. We both signed it. It was fair and amicable. He looked at me with tears in his eyes and said, if he couldn't have me as his wife, he wanted to be my friend at least.

Like the sucker I still was, I believed he was telling the truth.

9

CALL FOR REINFORCEMENTS

One moment we were hugging in the coffee shop, and the next, Mark reneged on our entire separation agreement and was demanding that I get my shit out of the house. I was at a loss. We had agreed, and the settlement was in his favor. He had told me I could keep my things in the house until I found a new place to live, so I didn't have to move it twice.

Now he had a fire under his ass to get me out of his life. If you've been through this before and come out the other side, you'll already know what happened. He found a new way to be in control, to appease his ego - he moved on. He found a new girlfriend. Just weeks after I had escaped our home, fearing for my safety, his pleading, his suicide threats, they all ended. I was no longer the apple of his eye, and he had someone new, exciting, to shower him with the attention he deeply desired. I was no longer needed, and everything he said in that coffeeshop about needing to be my friend was out the window.

He was back in control and out for blood.

Where he had been dragging his feet about signing papers, he now obtained a new lawyer and pleaded ignorance in signing our separation terms. He told his new counsel he didn't know what he had done, and now it didn't feel fair. We took the matter before a judge, and I lost. He lied, and I lost. He now wanted me to walk away with nothing and was prepared to spend the money on a lawyer instead of paying me out.

Our separation had been fair, really reasonable. I asked for half the equity in the home, and that is all. All of the things we had acquired since our marriage that I was entitled to – a $75,000 backhoe, a $25,000 side by side, a few snowmobiles, a new truck, alimony, everything – I was willing to leave behind. I had been making a meager salary when we were married, and although we split the bills 50/50, everything we did extra (which was a lot) Mark paid for because he had a much higher income than me. I didn't want any of it. I didn't want to include his family business; I just wanted enough to get out and start over. My dad disagreed with me and told me I would regret not going after everything he had. I was adamant that I wouldn't. I wanted to keep the peace, whatever element of peace there was.

Mark and I worked out one Saturday that I would come to pack up and move out my personal possessions. He conceded to let me leave all the furniture there, which was all mine, and he was letting me take it without a fight at least. He had ordered new furniture anyway, but it wouldn't be there for six weeks, so of course this "concession" was serving him well.

I felt good when I woke up that morning. I had my boxes organized, my trailer hooked up, and a plan in place. I would pack up the trailer room by room, with things I needed the least loaded up first and essential items like kitchen supplies loaded up last so that, when I did find my new home, everything would be easily organized and I could unpack in style.

As my truck was warming up in the driveway, he called.

"Your shit is all packed, so get over here and get it out of here now."

Excuse me?

"Get the fuck over here, and get your shit out. My mom and I packed it all yesterday, and it's in my way."

I don't remember what else was said because I lost my ever-loving mind. Mark yelled. I yelled. I screamed, and when I hung up, I cried. He had found a way to control the situation, yet again. Squeezing every ounce of his power over me, out of me.

I tore out of the yard, leaving my parents in the dust. They could meet me there; I was out for blood. He called me back on my drive, and I can't even remember the conversation. But whatever we screamed about put the fear of God in me again. I pulled over on the side of the road just a mile down from our home, called the RCMP, and told them I needed them there. I had to call the cops to get supervision to move out of my own home. They remembered me and our situation, advised me their ETA was 30 minutes and not to enter the house until they got there. I ignored their advice. I knew he wouldn't hurt me in front of his mom, and I knew she was there; I had heard her in the background, screaming her input on top of our arguing.

I blasted into the house, and it was worse than I had even thought. Piled up at the front door were masses and masses - of garbage bags. My clothes, all my books, office papers, trinkets, photo frames in garbage bags. Nothing labelled, in no particular order. I knew Mark was waiting to be happy with my reaction, so I turned on his mother, who was OCD about cleanliness, organization, and structure. She was also a decent human. She tried to defend her and her son's actions at first, but I had my best debate composure present by now, and I went toe to toe with her asked repeatedly if this is how she would want to be treated if she were in my position. I saw a tear come to her eye when she finally answered no, it was not.

My parents arrived by this time, and as soon as my mom walked in on the abomination, she spun on her heel and walked out, her fingers on fire, typing numbers in her phone. Within 60 minutes, the cops showed up, as did my own personal reinforcements. Two of my best friends, one of their boyfriends, my dad, my brother, five more trucks and two more big horse trailers. I was never going back – we were taking everything - today.

I have to admit; this was pleasing to watch and experience. As the cops stood guard beside Mark and his mom, he stood there doing nothing but watching as we loaded up "the convoy." If you've ever wondered, seven people can clear out a house in under an hour. The only time we hit a roadblock was when we would need something from Mark. When we needed his truck moved to get into the garage, he would see an element of control available, a fine line between refusing and knowing he can't because a cop is supervising him. He needed to "let it warm up," which he did for 15 minutes until the cop finally suggested, "I think you can move it now." He refused to let us use the backhoe to clear a path to the horse pens to collect my saddles, tack, arena equipment like barrels and jumps and panels. We had to trudge through 24" of snow and haul everything back by hand.

I'm not a vengeful person, but it was satisfying to see the house empty. He had nowhere to sit and no TV to watch and would remain that way for the next six weeks. I waved at his dad as our six trucks and three trailers packed to the roofs drove out slowly, one by one, passed his vehicle as he "sat guard" at the end of the driveway.

We all went back to my parent's house after, and mom made us a huge tray of nachos. I remember sitting around the table, bursting with gratitude for all the people who stopped and dropped everything about their day, and lent their backs and their trailers, which would now be storage units for my furniture until I found a new place to live. Maybe the best memory of all is when my friend's boyfriend, a dedicated cowboy, piped up, "Well, that was hard work. But I felt pretty good that near the end there when we were moving stuff out of the master bedroom. That was about the time the shit started melting off my boots."

And we laughed, and we laughed.

10

PHOENIX RISING

The phoenix holds symbolism in almost every spiritual teaching on earth, from Greek mythology, Chinese culture, Native American teachings, Celtic beliefs, and even in Christianity. As the story goes, near the end of its life, a phoenix settles on its nest of twigs and bursts into flames. From the ashes, a new phoenix rises. This rising symbolizes rebirth, hope, renewal, progress, the end of oppression, and eternity.

I erupted in flames. I had to resort to nothing, had everything stripped away from me, and I had two choices. To live in the ashes, or to rise again.

It would have been easy by this point to write off life. What had been so good about it anyway? My first love died, my rebound was a drug addict, and my husband had been an unfaithful, emotionally abusive alcoholic - and I wasn't even 30 years old. I had enough reasons to hate men forever and to think life sucked pretty bad. I could have lived in that nest of ash for the rest of my days, complaining and saying, "poor me", and living a mediocre life; I had the story to back it.

But instead, I chose to rise.

It took two years to finalize our divorce. In the end, I was awarded 1/3 less than what we had initially agreed to and spent half that final amount on legal fees getting it. The whole way through, my dad kept wanting me to fight for more, but I was not fond of the feeling inside of me, the person I would have to become to do that: malicious, greedy, argumentative, angry, vindictive, dirty. I reflected on my sessions with my counsellor, where she had me visualize walking around the farm that was ours, and if I had fought for it, how it would make me feel being there. Fighting tooth and nail for money gave me that same sickening feeling, so I stood my ground. By the time our final papers were signed, I was already rich.

Living back with my parents was extremely stressful for us all. I wasn't used to being accountable for my time when I would be home from work, how late I was staying out. They weren't used to me not being accountable to them, for when I last lived with them, I was "their child" beholden to their rules and regulations. Now I was an adult, someone who had been married, owned a house, and ran a corporate division. Why did I need to be accountable for what time I came home?! Our lifestyles just weren't jiving, and none of us were wrong for it. It was best for everyone that I move on. Blessedly, I found the perfect acreage for me. It's funny to look back on life, how I feared I would never have it as good as I did with my home with Mark. Was I ever wrong! If you are stuck in this place of thinking too, you, my friend, are also wrong! If we surrender, if we release control, if we believe in the good... if we rise... good we shall receive. Releasing Mark, the farm, the money, freed me to be blessed with what is rightfully mine in this world – beauty and abundance. Not only did I find an acreage for sale in the middle of our brutal Canadian winters, but I also found a property that was fully set up for horses, had the quaintest little farmhouse with the proverbial covered front porch, and it was on double the amount of land I had left behind! It was perfect.

Everything fell into place once I cut my ties with Mark and began standing on my own two feet. Not only was this acreage perfect, but its possession also was near-immediate, and my family and I only had to endure a total of six weeks of living together before me, Boo Roger, the cats, and my horses all moved to our new farm.

By this point, the phoenix had become incredibly symbolic to me, and I had one tattooed on my arm. Every morning when I woke up, I would stare at its beauty, channeling its strength. I was rising, almost ready to fly!

The story from here doesn't get as grand as that may sound, though... I was more like a baby phoenix, a fledgling, who left the nest a few days too soon. I surely hadn't learned all of life's lessons in those short six weeks. In fact, I immediately repeated the same pattern that I had with Mark and with Kent and started dating another alcoholic.

I don't like to make the same mistake twice. I like to make it three or four times – just to be sure.

Ugh. This time around, though, I saw it, and I saw it fast. We only dated four weeks instead of four years. Do you see universe? I'm learning! I may have fallen out of the nest, but my wings were strong enough to get me back up there, and I knew that's where I wanted to stay for a good long time.

Universal spirit works in unusual but very practical ways, bringing us life lessons to learn and learn, and learn again, until we finally get knocked over the head with a 2x4 and awaken. Or not. But I was committed to awakening. I was tested hard and fast, coming fresh out of the gates of divorce hell. I had a brief brush with another alcoholic, and then began online dating. I actually at one point was talking with three different Jason's at the same time. Keeping my text conversations in line with each of them was a test of its own, along with the resurgence of another blast from the past, one of Graham's other good friends, Nolan. The memory of the family friend, whose daughter fell in love with her boyfriend's best friend, came back to me once more. Maybe it was still for me, and I had just chosen wrong the first time! It's a sign!

We reconnected thanks to the power of social media. It turns out Nolan had always liked me too, and after Graham passed away, he tried to reach out, but Kent got to me first. Nolan and I started hanging out, but at the same time, I was also hanging out with the three Jason's. It got to the point where I had to choose. I liked Jason #2. A lot. He was hilarious, good looking, elusive, spontaneous, unreliable, and the exact type of emotionally unavailable mess I was most attracted to. The universe was trying to trick me! Test me! Well, my friends, I had learned. I chose Nolan. A proverbial good boy. Kind. Thoughtful. Vanilla.

Our relationship was - fine. He was lovely. I didn't love him. Neither of us said those three little words in the entire ten months we were together. I don't know if he felt it and didn't say it, but I definitely didn't feel it and I didn't say it. I was confused. I had learned my lesson, but was this the path I was meant to be on? I figured I had it wrong before and that passion and connection we all think is love is just a lusty farse, and we need to learn to love. Love more slowly and thoughtfully.

I'm sure this part of the story is entirely predictable. We got married.

JUST KIDDING. I broke up with him.

I was trying so hard to learn my lessons; why weren't they clear? Why did no one clap when I did it right? Where was the A+ on my report card for life? Why didn't I feel good about the break-up? What was love?

Remembering I like to make the same mistake several times, I did regret this decision about two months later. I tried to get him back, begged and pleaded, apologized to his family for breaking his heart, told him I loved him; we told each other we loved one another. We were able to fake it through this for about four months before he realized he didn't love me either, started becoming an ass, and dumped me on my birth-day. We never spoke again, but I did cancel my match.com subscription when the software brought him up as a 98% match for me a month later.

Some things had changed though, and I saw these mountains as just molehills. After the debacle that was my marriage, this was a cakewalk. I shook it off, moved on; it was time to go onward and upward.

Next mountain, please.

11

QUEEN OF THE CASTLE

As I continued to grow, not only did I forgive Mark, but I began to appreciate him. Because of him, I could do things alone. In our relationship, if something hadn't been important to him, it didn't get done. If it was important to him, I was instructed to be right there next to him so he could teach me. He was hard on me, and now that I was not in the relationship anymore, I was grateful for his harshness.

One day when I was still living on the farm with him, but we were separated, I needed to put out bales for the horses. I had a small boarding herd of about 11 horses or so, and we fed them with large round bales covered with "slow feed" nets so horses could "graze" as nature intended them to. They are fantastic inventions and give you weeks of no-chore feeding, but do require a form of "installation" to get them on.

It had been a particularly cold winter day after a good 12" of snow that, of course, blew in hard and drifted across the property. I got in Mark's backhoe and pushed and cleared and pushed and cleared the snow with the loader. And by pushed and cleared, I mean, dug the bucket too deep, ripped up ground, made a colossal mess, got stuck at least three times, and had to use the backhoe to pull myself out. Thank God he had disappeared somewhere to drink that day. I had been out in -40 for about four hours, and had successfully cleared the snow, gained access to the bale stack, put out and netted one bale and was on my last bale. The horses were hungry and not helping, but the net was frozen from the recent snow and the bale was falling apart before my eyes. There was no way I would get the net on it at this point, I was sure.

I called my dad, howling. "I'm so cold; it's so hard. Nothing is working." HOWWWWLLLLL. Of course, he immediately offered to come and help me; they only lived 15 minutes away. "NO," I remember saying.

"No. I have to do it alone."

"No, you don't," he said.

"Yes, I do." I straightened and wiped my tears. "Yes, I do. I want to live on a farm, and I will be living there myself. If I can't do everything that needs to be done, I have no business moving to my own ranch and having animals rely on my care. No. I will get it done."

And I did.

This event would foreshadow my life that was to come. I did it alone, all of it. I ran my farm, boarded horses, fixed the fence, put out the bales, and cleared the corrals. It wasn't all gravy; a lot of it was horrid. I remember sitting outside again in -40, bawling on the top of a bale, five feet in the air with a net I was trying to tighten the cord on to keep my horses alive and eating. Getting in and out and in and out of the tractor to move and shimmy bales so the nets would fit, opening and closing gates, having to be faster than the horses who wanted to escape from them, in and out, in and out. Ripping up more ground every time I touched the controls. I barely had yard grass at that farm, but it didn't matter because the horses were fed, and I had fed them.

I got myself in more than a few pickles; I remember another time I had borrowed my dad's side by side to haul delimbed trees and logs that had fallen on the property that I had chain-sawed up myself. I brought the ATV over in my brother's dump trailer, and it had two skinny ramps to unload from. My new farm was about 40 minutes from my family, so asking for help was a planned event. I could unload this machine; I believed I could do anything. I, at least, would try. But this was a little scary; I had to back the side by side down these skinny little ramps that, even at their closest placement, still only could fit half of each tire on the path. Here we go, and off we went, yep, right off the ramp. Holy shit. I leapt off the machine and watched it wobble on its frame, literally sitting half on and half off the trailer.

I looked around for help, but of course, there was no one there. Backing it any further meant sure disaster. It would fall on its side and ruin something, probably lots of things. This was not an option. Driving forward gave me a 50/50 chance of it still falling to the ground or righting back up into the trailer to try again (or just return the machine, unused, a story never to be spoken of). I knew I only had one option, and this time I wasn't calling dad to cry. So I went to the tack shed, put on my riding helmet, carefully climbed back in the side by side, did up the seat belt real tight, prayed, and hit the gas. We made it! I actually got it back on the trailer, and then swallowed all my fears from this near disaster and tried again, successfully this time! I whooped and hollered, and fist pumped and danced around the yard in victory. It was time to celebrate and get some farmgirl work done.

I have so many memories from those years on the ranch. I ran over a tree and got the skid steer stuck in the ditch of the driveway, and once I got my truck stuck in the middle of the grid road during a snowstorm. I was so shaken up from that event that I overshot my own driveway, pulling into it while trying to assess the scene, and drove off my own lane, getting stuck twice in one day. I had to resort to calling the neighbour to pull me out because no one else would dare try to travel during the storm we were having. Calling my own family for help took everything I had, so asking a near stranger for assistance was almost the death of me.

Another time, I was called home from work by a different neighbour; my horses were out and across the road after a windstorm broke a pasture gate. I became a master of my own Red Green sitcom… making random things fix stuff. Lead ropes, baling twine, proverbial duct tape, I even installed an underground electric boundary fence for my dogs by twisting the wires together with an eggbeater because I didn't have a drill.

Fallen trees on fence lines were no match for me and my 12" battery operated chain saw. I would saw and carve away divots for hours on a huge old tree that my little tool was no match for, but that tree was no match for me. I would hand auger and tamp in fence posts, even once building an entire corral fence by myself. I would hang 16-foot rails using a kitchen chair to hold up one end while I anchored the other end to the post. I would build dog gates out of pallets for Boo, rewire light fixtures, stain the deck, paint my room, prune the trees, haul and stack square bales, repair the shelters, and haul 5-gallon pails of water by hand from the house to the pens when the water bowl would freeze. There was nothing I wouldn't at least attempt to do, and most of what I tried, I succeeded at.

I chronicled all my adventures on social media and revelled in the attention people gave me. I was a superhero! Look at all these things a woman can do. I have one post saved, where dad had lent me his expensive lawnmower. He was quite nervous about me unloading it off the drop deck trailer and unstrapping the straps. I had, of course, told them about my success with saving the side by side on that last adventure. Everyone wanted to help, but I needed no help. I didn't want any help. I was Miss Independent. I brought the mower home, unstrapped it, unloaded it, and sent pictures to dad, showing him his precious piece of equipment was safe with me. He wrote back:

"You'll make someone a good husband one day."

Yes, yes, I will. I took care of myself, needed no one, and was damn proud of it.

I struggled those years, becoming stronger after each one, but I worked for it, earning my stripes. Not only with the physical chores of maintaining an 80-acre farm by myself, but also financially. Going from a double six-figure income to a single income, less than half of what we had lived healthily off of, was a shift. A big shift. A sacrificing shift.

I stopped getting my nails done. I learned to dye my own hair before quitting that altogether and letting my locks be whatever colour they wanted to be. I watched YouTube videos on how to trim and layer my mane. I haven't been to a salon for over seven years. Luxuries were not necessities, and I needed to afford fuel for my truck and feed for my horses. Hair was the last thing on my mind. Learning financial sacrifice was hard. I racked up my credit card on more than one occasion, not learning my lessons. I would have to sacrifice then even more and find something used to sell online to make up hundreds of dollars I had spent being sucked into online shopping, telling myself I deserved a new sweater every now and then. I did deserve a reward, but not as often as I shopped.

I wanted to make more money, but I already worked a full-time day job, plus my job keeping up the ranch maintenance and boarding horses. I needed and had always wanted a form of residual income; I made a few hundred dollars a month off my rental property in the city, but that wasn't getting me anywhere near the six-figure income that I was trying to replace. I had always been interested in direct sales, but I was not too fond of sales. Then I went to a home party one night and connected with the advisor. She sold jewellery, and I loved the entire catalogue. As farm-boy as I had become, I still had an obsession with jewellery. I set up a few calls with her and grilled her for hours about the opportunity. By this point in the story, you may have learned that new and improved Adelle does not take on a task unless she knows she can do it well.

So, the next phase in my life would be building an empire in direct sales and riding on the residual income wave for the rest of my life.

I bought the starter kit, booked my first few parties, of course begging my friends and family to be the hosts. I knew that to succeed I needed to get out of my warm market as soon as possible. I had never spoken publicly in my life, but my story and my goals and pitch rolled off my tongue. In the first two months of my business, I made it to the top ten sales leaders in Canada. Strangers booked parties with me, and I traveled to more homes, sold more jewellery, booked even more parties, took orders and earned. I earned cash, made every monthly incentive, and was promoted to a team leader in my first 90 days. I went to our national conference and a special team leader training and riverboat cruise and had built a team of advisers who were building their own teams. We were all earning and learning together. I learned how to sell by sharing; I was authentic about my business and faced many, many a fear I had about putting myself "out there" for people to judge. I was doing this because I loved and believed in it, and I was amazingly accessorized doing so.

Unfortunately for me and many of my fellow advisors, the company foreclosed ten months after I had started. I earned over $1500 a month extra doing less than one party a week. It wasn't the lottery, but it was only the start. I had grown rich in experience, fully embraced the power and ability of direct sales, but I also wanted more. Being exceptional in direct sales was coined as "being the best copycat" to the person before you. This is true and why it provides such a clear pathway to success for anyone to achieve. But at the same time, I wanted to do something that was mine, all mine. I didn't know what yet, but I was on my way.

I felt unstoppable. I was making it on my own. I had made it. I hadn't dated in years - actual years. I was learning my lessons, manifesting the shit out of everything I wanted, and my next relationship was going to be my ride or die. It had to be perfect, and it had to be someone who was their own whole person. I had lists of skills and expectations. Outdoorsy, independent, affectionate, self-sufficient, funny, could dance, oh, the list went on (there was actually a physical list). It was that, or nothing for me, because I didn't NEED anyone. I had to want them. This feeling of power over my next relationship after leaving Mark was so refreshing. I was going to do it right this time, and it would be for forever.

12

MY CINDERELLA STORY

After my divorce, I always said that I was going for a love like the movies or bust. That I would hold out for that kind of undying love.

Every time I watched a romantic movie, I could FEEL it. The soulmate's eyes meet from across the room - instant connection at first sight: undeniable chemistry, unbridled passion, true love. By this point in time, I was a few years out from my divorce and was doing pretty okay in my life. I was fiercely independent, able-bodied, killing it on a single income, and loving it. So, if someone wasn't going to come in and turn my life upside down with a love like the movies, I had better things to do.

I was living my best life and for the past few years had helped my friends at local tradeshows in western Canada promote their TV show. It was fun and exciting to get away and do something different than work an office job by day and chore on the farm by night. I would meet new people, sell some T-shirts, hang with my friends, and maybe, just maybe, find my soulmate.

I had been to a few shows at this point, but no luck yet. Then in April of

2015, we packed up and headed out for another fun-filled trade show weekend.

Jack and I have two different starts to our story. That is because he saw me first. I did not see him until the following day. Later, as we exchanged stories, he recalled seeing me setting up the tradeshow booth and said he loved me then. "Your hair was half-up, and you had on a leather jacket and thigh-high boots." Well, if you knew me at that point in my life, it was unmistakably my style. I didn't see him until the banquet after the first day of the tradeshow. I was sitting with some other people that I knew less well at the time. My TV friends were considered pretty famous in this setting, so they were sitting at the head table. All through supper, I had no one to bounce the excitement of the eye contact made with this gorgeous creature off of. It kept happening. I'd glance up, over to the next row of tables and down about three. And I'd see him already looking. Sometimes I'd look first, and he'd catch me back.

After the main course was served, I couldn't contain my excitement anymore. People got up and started to mingle a bit, refresh their drinks before the evening program. I got up and went to Heidi at the head table. I crept over to her, and we discussed in hushed excitement this new mystery man. Nope, she didn't recognize him either. This was an excellent first indication because they know everyone in the industry, and if they didn't know him, maybe he was actually single. Every available man they cumulatively knew they had already tried to set me up with.

She agreed, so handsome. What are we going to do next? We continued to whisper, but not so quietly that her outspoken, extroverted, well-intending husband, who had returned to the table and was hovering over his seat I was occupying overheard. "What? A boy? Who? Where." Heidi, also well-intending, immediately pointed out the mystery hunk while I did the classic tuck and roll under the table.

Undeterred, excited, and with good intentions, Heidi's husband, Derek, marched directly over to his table. At the same time, Heidi and I tried to look like we were having a fabulous time and I had just told an incredibly funny joke (insert hair toss here) while we side-eyed the scenario to try and watch what was going on.

The story is even better than just your classic love story because Heidi and Derek's dynamic are "famous" in this industry. I use "famous" in quotations because they simply aren't famous to me - they are my best friends. They deserve to be called famous without the quotes, as in all of Canada and the US, they have a top 10 show in their industry. I'm so proud of them, but they're still just my people to me.

Anyway, the fact that Derek is famous and is walking up to some random table – these lucky people – are visibly excited. I sneered at Heidi and said, "Well, hell. When he goes over there, and they realize he's not there for autographs, but an introduction for a girl, they're going to be so deflated."

You could just see the group's eyes light up. Here he was, this star, coming to their table. He walks straight up to Mr. Handsome, sticks out his hand and says, "Hi. I'm Derek. Are you single?" We could literally watch the confusion cross their faces. Derek is happily married to one of the most beautiful women on the planet, with a bouncing baby boy they adore, who in years to follow, would have a lovely little sister complete their family. Quick-witted as Derek is, he recognized his word choice error and recovered. "No – not me. My friend. A girl. Let me rephrase. Are you single - and straight?"

The next hour is a blur. All I remember was the mystery hunk was indeed single, and the next thing that I recall is standing in front of him awkwardly by the bar while Derek officially introduced us. We made awkward small talk over a drink, and when the banquet was wrapping up, our group planned to go to the local pub. Derek, who has always been my greatest wing-girl, extended the invitation for Jack to join us.

Sitting together at the after party, I looked around the table at the now multiple famous TV personalities. *Ahhh*, I thought as the night went on, Jack is just here for these connections. Feigning interest in me to get to them. What a jerk.

The night ended un-climactically (literally and figuratively), and I went back to my cabin, unsure of what would transpire, and wondering what his true intentions were.

What did transpire? My utter Cinderella story. He must have read the script. Jack came calling for me the next day at the booth; my friends and I squealed like schoolgirls after he left. Then I called on him (I'm all about equality you know) and got his number.

We texted back and forth in the weeks after the show, and the next thing I knew, he was coming through my city for a trip and promised to stop in on his way home.

Except he didn't. He didn't stop, and he didn't call.

So what was I to do?

Not meek anymore, I called him out on it. I started off innocently asking him how his trip went, and when he replied that it was pretty dull and uneventful, I remember sneering, saying something like, I was sorry his trip didn't go the way he planned, but at least he still had his thumbs. Yikes.

My snark got the conversation rolling, and from there, he was open and honest with me. He just didn't know how to tell me at first, so he said nothing.

As our conversation evolved, he shared with me the truth. Just before he had left for his trip, his ex-girlfriend came back.

She was pregnant. They were going to try to make it work.

Right before my eyes, my Cinderella story went up in smoke. By this time, I was used to dusting off the ashes, but this one did hurt. I respected the man he was for making that call. We stayed Facebook friends, and I watched him from afar. Appropriately "liking" a predetermined number of posts and photos each week, ensuring not to give away the fact that, not only did I see everything he posted, but I would also go back in the archives and stare at his photos, his family's photos, screenshotting many of them to send back to Heidi along with my woes.

I watched their maternity season blossom. I'm sure I was the first to know when they posted the bouncing baby boy was born; I watched as they appeared happy and making it work. I would post things of me being outdoorsy and fun to entice him to like my posts. It worked. But we never did more than a like back and forth.

I didn't meet anyone else.

Then one day, or closer to like, 480 days, I was travelling back home after my annual "Solo in SoCal" vacation, and I was stuck in Calgary. My flight was postponed and postponed. As I was lying on an airport recliner in exhaustion, for the first time in over a year and a half, he randomly did more than a Facebook like. He snap-chatted me. He was driving to Saskatchewan. What. He lived near Calgary, and I lived in Saskatchewan, and our paths were mixed right up! We chatted for a moment or two, and then, my flight got cancelled. It was 11:30 pm, and I was already supposed to be home. The farm sitter was gone. They wanted to put us up in a hotel and fly us out at 11:30 the next morning.

So I did what any forward-thinking female would do. I rented a car, drove all night, and was in my bed by 7:30 am. I woke up the next day, happy and snuggling with my doggos with no regrets, and I'd do it again (actually, I wouldn't. It was -50 with howling winds, a horrible drive I split with a stranger, and I was exhausted). But this time, I was home, and it was another frigid winter day, so... pyjamas all day! No makeup, hair wild, binge-watching tv - then at 5:00pm, Jack snapped me again. He was in my city for the night and wanted to meet. I was exhausted and unprepared to see anyone, let alone the love of my life who was ripped away from me and now wants to be friends. As Jack and I were snapping back and forth, I was texting Heidi on the side, letting her know the play by play. She encouraged me to go. So I probably shouldn't go. But I guess I'll go; it would be nice to have another friend.

It took us all night to get down to the brass tax. I went to town, and we went for dinner. We talked in circles about our lives and our truths. I was too afraid to ask about his son and his partner, he didn't bring them up either. After supper, he was supposed to have heard from his cousin who he was staying with. But his cousin was "ghosting" him. Could he come to hang out at my place for a while? I was unclear on his intentions, but upon agreeing to him coming over I was already calling him an asshole in my head, planning out what I would do in the event he made a move on me and stepped outside his relationship.

I agreed to let him come over. I felt bad he had nowhere else to go. As I climbed in my truck, with Jack following behind, I speed dialled Heidi to update her with what was transpiring.

"HE IS COMING TO YOUR HOUSE?!"

"Yes. But we are just friends."

I think it took another hour… when his cousin still hadn't called him back, it was nearing 11 pm, and he still had no place to stay. "Well, you can sleep in the spare room, but how will your girlfriend feel about that?" I sneered as I walked away into the kitchen

"I don't…." He was still talking, but I couldn't understand him.

"You don't what?" I couldn't hear him.

"I don't have a girlfriend."

Oh.

They tried to make it work. He stuck it out for 18 months. But here he was, my prince, in my living room, single.

I had to work the next morning and had driven all night from Calgary to get home after my missed flight. What was a girl to do?

I set him up in the spare room and went to bed.

13

#FIVEPERCENTING

Jack and I started a long-distance relationship after that night. When he left in the morning, we hugged the biggest hug, and it was gut-wrenching to watch him drive out the driveway – leaving my life just as soon as he had re-entered it.

We were as joined at the hip as two people living 300 miles apart could be, constantly texting, calling, snapping… but it was still all on the down-low. Heidi and Derek knew on my end, and that was it. I don't even think anyone on his end knew because, as excited as we both were for this resurrected chance at a life together, he still had some responsibilities to sort out. The mother of his child was living in the master bedroom of his home and he was sleeping on the couch. Their relationship was over – but he was never anything other than a gentleman, wise beyond his years, and she had no job, no vehicle, nowhere to go, so she stayed.

He would make the trek to my farm every second weekend, and it stayed that way for months. I believe our first Facebook official photo was a post I made on my birthday four months later, being grateful for "the man who loves me long distance."

I remember the first time I went to his home in the badlands of Alberta. I packed up a truck full of 3 dogs and headed west. I was so nervous, excited, scared, and in love. This would be my future home. There had never been a discussion of who moves where, but it was an unspoken agreement that it would be me going. He had a son. The son's mother lived in the same town; Jack's parents and brothers lived close by. It made sense. Plus, our home was beautiful. Well, the land was beautiful, the house needed work, but we had grand plans. We lived in the mouth of a 160-mile-long coulee into the heart of the badlands. Literally the backyard was our oyster. Many mornings after coffee, we would strap on our boots and head out to explore. Each trip was a new adventure. We had hoodoo's and caves and creeks in our own backyard. We hunted for dinosaur bones after fresh rainfall, never coming home without bones and teeth and other skeletal parts that we would wash up and try our best to figure out which species of ancient creature it would have been from, imagining the days that dinosaurs roamed the land we called our home.

The dogs were living in dog-heaven-on-earth. They had hills and valleys to roam, a creek to cool off in, a step-fur-dad who loved them as if they were his own. Jack was the most selfless, generous human being I have ever met.

We would spend our bi-weekly visits together making plans to make his home - our home. We would stake out the future garage with the loft above it that would become his hunting museum and outfitters office. We would mow the grass and draw out the firepit area with a swinging loveseat and plan how we would pull back the landscape that would open the backyard and sweep down to the creek which ran past the house not 50 yards from the back door. When I close my eyes, I can still feel myself lying in bed cuddling with Jack on an early morning, listening to the creek roar from the spring runoff from the coulee tops melting in full force. We planned the most expansive horse pastures, riding arena, barn, petting zoo… We dreamed the good dream.

Our time together was always an adventure. After spending two weeks apart at a time, each of us working full-time jobs plus managing our acreages, our weekends were our respite. It was nothing but fun and adventure. When he would come here, we would travel to the apple orchard, picnic by the cover of the oldest tree in the province while the rain poured down around us, we would hike my land and the prairies for antler sheds.

We spent hot July afternoons in the badlands by the river, swimming with the dogs at our little private launch just 3 miles from the house. Jack would throw sticks for the dogs until there were no more sticks to be had on the beach. We would have to go home and come back the next day, wait and hope that the river would bring more throwing sticks to chase.

After a morning of drinking coffee and dreaming our homestead plans, an afternoon of badlands hiking followed by a river cool off, he would cook (yes, he did the cooking – I still don't cook at this phase of my life) a most delicious supper, and then after supper, we would go for a drive. Sometimes we stayed down in the valley; others, we climbed the winding roads up out of the valley and scoured the coulee tops for signs of big game animals before hunting season. We drove. We would slam on the brakes and detour off the highway to catch a photo of an owl. We would sit parked in silence, glassing a pea field looking for deer with our binoculars. Other days, we would get up at 5 am and head to the wildlife preserve where he would bugle in an elk so I could photograph their incredible beauty. I recall the dew still burning off the grass, the morning dead silent, where we would feel the rumble from the earth from this majestic animal galloping towards us before we could even see him.

We lived. We loved. We thrived.

We had such extraordinary times together that we came up with our own hashtag.

We called it #fivepercenting.

Every photo we posted, every story we told, every experience we had together, we would look at each other and smile and say, "I love five-percenting with you."

We felt that we were living, loving, like only 5% of the world might get to experience.

The afternoons of our inevitable departures away from each other, back east for me or west for him, those long 300 miles, separated us for the next fortnight; we would sit on the loveseat, looking across at each other, our legs intertwined, our hands held tightly together, look each other deep in the eyes, and recant how we met, how we felt that day— meeting eyes across the room. What we felt and how our breath caught when our stare was returned. We shared our innermost feelings that each of us experienced when we saw each other for the first time. He knew he needed to meet me. I knew he was the most handsome man I had ever laid eyes on.

Recalling these memories kept our love alive. It kept our passion thriving. It was the key. No matter how many times we told each other our rendition of the story over and over again, I never got tired of hearing it. It ignited a flame inside me that kickstarted my will power to spend the next two weeks without him. Thinking about our story pacified all the hurt and longing I had for him while we were apart. The missing, the pain, the desire to have him near me... It was the lifeline to our relationship. I think when couples fall out of the practice of reminding themselves, or each other, why they fell in love is when love starts to die.

———

Looking back, it sounds so perfect. It makes me both smile with the joy of the memory and weep for the pain of its loss.

Was it reality? Could my Cinderella story have felt like that forever? It's supposed to. It's what I'd been holding out for. It was love like the movies or bust. People would ask me, would that be what it was like when we lived together full time? Well, we lived that way for an entire year, both working more than full time, doing multiple jobs, managing two acreages, and then every second weekend was like an extended date night.

Why couldn't that be the norm? It would be our norm. We would show the world how to five percent.

14

MILES APART

Jack and I became one in every sense of the word. We lived 300 miles apart, but that was the only thing that separated us. We loved all of the same things; we were on the same page. We could communicate – like, honestly communicate. We could read when the other person was off and talk through how it affected us both and what we could agree to do to improve.

Looking back, our demise all started when I began to prefer to go to his farm versus having him come to mine. So subtle, right? For a time, I was able to talk myself into the fact it even made sense. I would be moving there, so why not spend the majority of our time there? I loved my acreage and was grieving giving it up – so distancing "us" from my farm – seemed appropriate and rational on my part.

Except it wasn't feasible for me to go there every weekend or second weekend – we were both working full time, and with a 5-hour drive on a Friday night after work, and a 2 pm departure on a Sunday, it left us with a whole 24 waking hours together. It was a lot of travel, not to mention the cost. We were both single incomes living on our acreages, and our living costs were high. Adding $500 a month in fuel to travel to and fro quickly became a budgeted item that came with other expenses being cut as a sacrifice to be together.

That meant he had to come to my home too. Our weekends at my farm became more strained. I didn't revel in his anticipated arrival. Before he even would walk in the door, I began to count down two sleeps and look forward to when he would leave so I could starfish in my king size bed by myself. I love sleeping alone. I still actually do not understand why people suffer through having terrible nights of sleep just to lie next to your mate so you can elbow each other to stop snoring, or to move over, sleep shitty, waking up at each other cranky, when you could have a beautiful separate sleep, wake up happy, pop in the next room (brush your teeth first) and snuggle up to your honey as a sweet good morning after a rested and refreshed sleep. I think it could save marriages if we could get a good night's rest. But whatever, I get it – I'm the weirdo – story of my life. Moving on. Sleeping together was important to Jack, so we did, and he was the best sleeping partner I have ever had. Didn't snore, didn't toss and turn, and literally would contort his body into any shape as not to disturb the dogs who also slept on the bed with us.

But still. I began to resent his arrival, and it did not go unnoticed. As much as I had evolved from my early days of being a bad friend, I was still pretty poor at hiding my personal feelings well. Life is just too short to pretend you're having a good time if you're not. So, he would notice. At first, he just sucked it up and didn't say anything. Then I noticed how he wasn't himself, then I felt terrible, so I would bring it up.

It was getting to the point where we were making the call and planning me moving to his home. It was fall, time for a major yard cleanup, and instead of putting things away, we began moving outdoor things like planters and patio furniture to his house instead of my shed.

Through this process, I began to not see how our lives would work once we lived together. I had allowed other people's opinions to get in my head. We had spent a year dating long distance, and when we were together on our weekends, we were TOGETHER. Whether regular or long weekends, we were glued to each other's hip for the 24 or 48 hours we had. We had been dating so long that yes, I still loved him and everything about him, but I was also comfortable with him, and with me, and with our individuality. I started having thoughts like - *do we have to do EVERYTHING together? How would this work when we lived in the same house?*

I couldn't see the forest through the trees, and it began to freak me out. My three favorite pastimes are bird watching, photography, and horses. As time went on, Jack started putting up bird feeders in his yard at home, sitting on the deck with his binoculars like I did every weekend morning and would send me photos of the new species arriving now that he had food and water out. Then, he started sending me pictures of cameras to buy because he wanted to start taking photos too. I felt a little quirky but talked myself down. It only made sense with his intended hunting business that he would have a camera; I soothed my nerves with my rationality. *No big deal, Adelle.* Then, he bought his own horse. A triple threat, the three things that defined "me" were now things that would be "ours." I felt myself, the me I had worked so hard to be, slipping away.

I began to get silently resentful and hid it (not well). The debater in me switched from her affirmative position to the opposition. He had his hockey. I wasn't signing up for hockey so we could be together every minute of the day. He went to his games, and sometimes I would see myself going and others I wouldn't. I'd support his hobby but not encroach in his personal time for it. I felt that as two whole people, we needed hobbies that we did without each other. I wasn't taking up being a hunter. Sure, I loved going scouting in the evenings with him – sometimes. But there were many, many times that he would go hunting alone. When we blended our hobbies is when I felt we bonded. I would bring my camera and take photos of the deer he was scouting. He would teach me about the deer, and I would teach him about the camera. It was sharing, without overtaking. He was the expert in one, and I in the other. Coming together brought value that we could both contribute to each other.

Then when he bought a horse, I snapped inside. What would I ever do by myself? My independence was burning up faster than I could stoke the fire. I was terrified. So, I began to blame him. I told myself HE was not confident, so he leaned on me and tried to be like me, and I NEEDED someone who was independent and their own person. I couldn't be a crutch.

I started to put that perspective on everything he did. Telling myself that he lacked confidence and was trying to please me. It frustrated me, and he began to annoy me. It became easier to blame him than understand I had built up some pretty strong walls around my heart, life, and independence (and rightfully so – considering my baggage from Mark that I never actually unpacked well).

Now, when it was getting to the push comes to shove stage... putting my farm up for sale and moving west... that I began to look for excuses to run.

It didn't help that his parents didn't like me. I couldn't understand it; parents have always liked me. Breaking up with boyfriends has always been a tedious and grief-filled process, mainly because I drag it out as I mourn the loss of the family I had gained. But in this instance, it was different. At first, I couldn't figure out why. So I used it as more gasoline on my slow burn to disaster, saying to myself, do I really want this dynamic for my in-laws? Was I about to move to a new province, become a stepmom, and have his parents down the road who make me uncomfortable and dislike me? It was a good argument. I know many people don't get along with their in-laws, but I wanted it all: my Cinderella story, the prince, and his fabulous family.

Oh, hindsight, you are always so clear. Looking back, I realize two things were going on. One was that Jack was growing into the person he was meant to be. He was always so sensitive and giving to others at all costs, including his mental health. He struggled to speak his truth for fear of disappointing someone. This was an uncomfortable process for everyone involved, and when a person begins to build healthy boundaries, the people who mourn them not being there anymore start to push back. But Jack didn't deserve that. He was growing and flourishing, genuinely listening to his inner self, and what he wanted in life was becoming clear instead of muddled with other people's opinions. So that being said, because it was so hard for him to stand up to his parents, I began to meddle in things I shouldn't have.

He was in a tough spot. Looking back, I would change so much, but instead, I will learn and do better for the future. Once we were deep in development planning around his acreage, I realized that there was one spot he was kind of avoiding discussing development. But it was the perfect spot for a barn. Trying as he might to keep everyone happy... he had failed to disclose that the reason he was able to purchase this property in the first place was that his parents had given him a large sum of money, with the intention that they were part property owners, and once they retired, would be moving from the city to the country... and building a second house on that land.

To say I was shocked would be an understatement. I don't want to live anywhere near my own family, let alone my gained family, who disliked me, I was not okay with this. Already I was moving 300 miles away from the only home I had ever known, was downsizing from my 80-acre property to 40, leaving all my friends, all my family, my career, I was going to become a stepmother to a toddler, and live on the same property as my in-laws? I couldn't do it.

I don't know even now, many years later, what the perfect recipe to this all would have been to make it a success. But what I did do that I know was wrong - was have this conversation for Jack, with his parents. We had many discussions about it, and deep down, he didn't want it to happen either, but before he met me, his single income precluded any other option. Give and take, and he would have sacrificed living with his parents to stay on the property. But now, things had changed. We would be a double-income family, and with the sale of my property, we could buy them out of their investment. This is what Jack said he wanted. But he was so afraid to have the conversation and disappoint them that I offered to do it and take the blame.

Huge gigantic mistake. Highly unrecommended. Now Jack's parents really did hate me. I was uprooting and disrupting their retirement plan, which – rightfully so - I understand entirely the upset this would cause. But the root of it all, was that was not a conversation I should have been having. We were rushing, Band-aiding, patching a leak. They had sold their house in the city and were literally living IN Jack's house. On the weekends I would come to visit, they would pack a bag and stay with his sister so Jack and I could have some time alone. They were homeless, and now I was taking away their retirement dreams. What a nightmare.

I had two options, to dig in or run.

15

MOONING ON

Were the cards stacked against us? Was it a sign? Was this really Cinderella and Prince Charming, Romeo and Juliet? I wanted a love like that. But what I forgot was the middle of the movie, where the couples faced extreme difficulty first before ending up together.

Jack was one of the best humans I have ever known. When we were together, I wanted him to be everything he had the potential to be. But when he started to grow into that person, he found his truth and inner voice. He began to have an opinion and the confidence to talk about it. Suddenly, my world was turned upside down. Whereas everything we did before had been my idea – how we would landscape, decorate – now he was chiming in. I was not fond of the things we started to disagree on. I wasn't in full control anymore. As he began to feel comfortable being the person I always saw in him and wanted him to be, I suddenly had a problem with it. Before, he would do anything to please me, and now he would share if something was significant to him, even if I didn't like it. I had no sense of balance. I see now that I had rebounded too far from being oppressed under Mark's control, over-compensating and becoming the controlling one.

Instead of realizing my negative coping strategy and protection method, not seeing how many walls I had built up, I took it as more fuel that we were growing apart and weren't meant to be together.

It also didn't help that my family wasn't all that supportive either. For me to be with Jack, I would have to move to a different part of the country. I understand their hesitation. What parent wants their only daughter to live a days' worth of travel away? I imagine that the most challenging task of being a parent is to want your kids to be what THEY want to be when they grow up, not what you want them to be.

They "said" the right things, but I could tell in their passive tones they didn't mean them. I must get my inability to hide my true feelings from them. They poked holes in our story. Initially, I planned to rent out my acreage, with the theory that it would give me some time to grieve the loss of the home where I had found myself after my divorce. No way no how they said. It would be way too much work, and if it gets run down, it will depreciate in value. Nope, get rid of it if you're going to go. This stopped me in my bag-packing tracks. What if it didn't work out, and I needed to move back home? This property was incredible and more than I had ever dreamed I would have. It was my liberation, restart, independence, and proof that I could do hard things and move on with my life after leaving Mark.

This began to eat away at me. Doubt crept in. Not having the full love and support of your family to make one of the most significant decisions of your life was paralyzing. I felt the looming season of spring, which would be the ideal time to list a real estate property, leaning down on me, and I began to retreat into my fortress of safety.

Looking back, I see many alternatives. We could have deferred moving in together for a year or six months even. We could have continued to commute long distance; we had only been dating one year at this point. It would have been more than reasonable. We could have rented the property against my parents' advice. I could have moved there temporarily for the summer. I didn't recognize that the control Jack's parents had over him was the same as mine had over me. In addition to the farm, there were smaller actions his parents would take against me.

At Christmas, we had been waiting to have an alternative day celebration, one when Jack had his son. On Boxing Day, the waterbowl in my horse's corral froze over meaning I was now tied to the farm. Later that day, it was decided their Christmas get together would occur on the next. I felt it was planned reactively out of spite that I wasn't able to be there, and Jack didn't stand up for me and tell his parents he wanted to wait. In turn, being frustrated that he didn't have the guts to say hard things to his parents was me being frustrated with myself for not having the courage to say hard things to my parents. I didn't recognize that I was just like him.

We had a love that should have withstood all of these obstacles if we had been able to come together. It would have been hard, no doubt. Romeo and Juliet hard. But we could have made it.

Instead, when it got difficult, I did what I had started to do best the last few years - I left.

I knew I was leaving well before I left. I have always shied away from small changes. Do not move the furniture in the house, the trinket, the painting. When I do change, it is significant. Sell a vehicle, get a new one, go from blonde to black, chop off my waist-length hair to a bob, sell my farm that I had grieved leaving in order to be with Jack, and buy a new one.

Come again?

Yeah, you read that right. The sticking point I had about moving to a new province was leaving my farm. And here I was not even broken up with Jack yet, looking at moving to an even bigger, better new farm. How twisted is that? It's twisted. I read this chapter over and over, saying to myself, *I need to expand the transition.* It's literally Jack, then moving to a new farm. Unfortunately, though, this is how the story goes. I was looking at the property before I even broke up with Jack. I could have used this as motivation and proof to myself that I could cut ties with my old farm and enjoy a new home and life with Jack in Alberta. But by this time, I was gone, long gone from our relationship. I have no other excuse and no filler to break this part of the story apart.

I needed a distraction for the loss of this great love that I hadn't even left yet. I decided if I wasn't moving west that it was time to invest in my property and build a barn. I began researching cost and told my family this was what I was determined to do. They were a bit rattled too. I think because, although they had beat the clock on me moving far away, I was now going to root down on the opposite side of the city from them, something they also didn't love because I was still so far away. It was round trip of over an hour to get to my place, so if I was in dire need of help, it didn't come very fast.

Needless to say, before this whole interprovincial move, my parents had been trying to get me to think about moving closer to them and my brother, who lived two miles apart. I love my family but having just left a relationship because my in-laws would be living too close – I was wary. Oh, the irony. Trust me – I get it. One day my dad called me into his office and said, "Hey, look at this place!" We had done this dog and pony show before, and there was always something monumentally wrong with his prospective choice of ranches. Plus, my current farm was not easy to beat, so before I even glanced over, I said, "I am not moving - to anywhere but there."

It. Was. Perfect.

A beautiful home, fully landscaped yard, trees, pasture, 80 acres, it was everything I already had.

Plus, all the things I didn't already have. A heated shop and a barn.

It was closer to my parents, but still 10 miles from them, past theirs from town. So it was not a convenient "stop in unannounced" location they could drop into on their way home from the city. It would be an intentional drive, and even if they called me as they were leaving their driveway, I still would have 12 minutes to prepare.

At this time, I had begun really getting connected with universal law and unconditional love. I had toyed with it since about my mid 20's, going to energy work clinics for horses, and my first big awakening to it was after reading Lynn Grabhorn's book, *Excuse Me Your Life is Waiting*. She took the power of The Secret and connected the dots for me. Her messaging about the vibe, the feeling, the satisfaction of already having the thing you were trying to manifest had been the piece I was missing. After reading her book, I manifested things here and there, good parking spots, time left on the meter, money, etc.

But manifesting a new farm would take a lot more intention than anything I'd focused on before, and I needed more education. The month before, I had on a whim ordered about seven self-help books, and I read every one of them. The one that stood out was *The Universe Has Your Back* by Gabby Bernstein. Where Lynn had talked about feeling and vibing the "thing" already in your life, Gabby taught about surrender. That you can feel and work towards the manifestation of anything, but then you need to surrender. You have to do all the work to manifest and then release control of the outcome. What you want may come to you the way you thought it would, or in a completely different way, or maybe not at all. This was a pivotal point to what I had been missing in my early energy work, and I was ready to take it to the next level.

Gabby teaches about asking the universe for signs, so I whispered to my mom as we toured this new property that I was looking for an owl as a sign this place was meant for me. I hadn't seen one inside the house yet and was getting a bit worried. She replied, "Are you kidding me? Didn't you see the owl statue out the patio window in the raspberry garden?"

Oh. Well, then.

My next big task was releasing control. I am a control freak. I am a planner, a Type A, and like to be in control at all times, please. Somehow, I came across literature about manifesting with the phases of the moon. Most of us know about the power of a full moon and how people can get a little crazy during it, but we can also use the whole moon cycle for manifesting, and I decided to give it a go to see if I could buy this farm.

I began praying daily to the universe (you can pray to the Universe, God, Creator, Angels, Love, Spirit, it is all the same to me, and I use them interchangeably) to help me release control of the outcome of having a barn. Sounds a bit complicated, I know. It wasn't to say I was giving up the possibility of having a barn; I just released where and how it would come to fruition. Maybe it would come now, or perhaps it would come in ten years. If the new beautiful place was not meant for me, the universe would steer the opportunity away from me and open a different window of opportunity to have a stable, at some point. My test was to remain trustful of the outcome and not try to control the process.

So I prayed for peace and strength to support me through surrender. As the new moon arrived, I set my intention:

"I have a barn, live close to the river on lots of land, with my horses, donkeys, dogs, and cats. I release control of the outcome to the universe and pray for my angels' support when my faith wains. I love, believe, and trust in the universe, Amen."

Manifestation isn't about just getting lucky. It's about doing the work and releasing control of the outcome. You don't just get to sit back and have things delivered to your doorstep. You have real work to do. For me to get a new farm, I had to sell my old farm. And like most other home-owning humans, those little projects on the "one freaking day" list now needed to be done, today. The energy to do them came out of nowhere. The contractors for painting and repair were magically available in two days time due to their other job being cancelled. Things were happening at a pace I was in disbelief of.

After a new moon, the first quarter is time to work hard, dig in, and take action towards your goal while still surrendering. It's an art. As I was getting the home reno's underway, we made a conditional offer on the new farm, and I released control of the outcome of it being accepted.

As this was all happening, I had been long booked to speak at a national event in Ottawa that would take me through the full moon – the high time for moon magic. My farm got listed the morning I was booked to travel, and before I got on my first connecting plane, there were four showings booked that day.

Releasing, surrendering, and trying to focus on work was quite the task. That evening, I was out with a co-worker in a quaint little downtown Ottawa restaurant. My phone kept incessantly dinging and buzzing in my purse to the degree that I could not ignore. I picked up my phone and saw multiple missed calls, texts, and voicemails from my mom, dad, brother, and realtor. The first text I opened said, "CALL ME BACK. THERE IS A FULL PRICE OFFER, AND IT EXPIRES AT MIDNIGHT!"

My surrendering was working. The offer on the new farm wasn't accepted yet, so essentially, I was now homeless. Single, heartbroken, and homeless. How ironic. What was a girl to do – except surrender some more.

16

THROUGH THE REAR VIEW

I could barely believe it. My surrender to intention meant that by the end of the moon cycle, the new farm was mine. I was so busy with the move, settling into my new castle, and expanding my equine business that I didn't even realize that I missed Jack. It hit me like a ton of bricks. I had started working with a therapeutic horse wear company doing product development, marketing, and communications. Although I worked mostly from home, I travelled there once every six weeks for a few days at a time. I had never been to the town they were located, and I was initially comforted when I realized that 90% of the trip was down the same highway I could travel with my eyes closed - to Jack's. This seemed comforting until I hit the road.

It was the peak of summer just two months after I had moved and six months after I had ended our relationship. As I turned on to that quiet secondary highway that extended into quiet peaceful stretch of travel, I felt the first pang of regret. As the landscape changed and I passed the familiar farmyards that crept towards the badlands, it almost broke me as I made that last turn. If I had kept going straight at the fork in the road, I was only 30 miles away from my past life. A beautiful drive that would in an instant drop me from the top of the prairies down to the heart of the badlands. It was tempting. I was so close. Maybe I could just drive by? Instead, I took the detour south to my exciting new job, but I couldn't shake the thought of him. Of us. Why was I suddenly feeling this way? I had made the right call. Had I made the right call?

I couldn't shake the thought of him. We hadn't talked since the breakup, and he had blocked me on social media. I couldn't settle my upset and extended an olive branch with a text, letting him know I had just travelled down our highway and was filled with good memories. He replied hours later, with a simple, "yeah," clearly not extending the branch back so I wrote, "good times," and left it at that.

Except as the days passed, I couldn't leave it at that. I replayed our relationship over and over in my head. I walked through our times of trouble, which I began to realize were my times of trouble. He had been a rock-solid partner, always there for me, waiting, extending himself beyond reason to connect with me. And instead of letting my guard down, instead of dropping the bridge to allow him into the fortress I had built, I kept him outside the castle to pine for me as the prince for Rapunzel. Except I was both Rapunzel and the witch, and I cut myself off from him because it was starting to feel too real, too scary, too vulnerable.

I was an idiot. I regretted my decision and blamed myself heavily. I realized that I hadn't felt safe letting him in. After Mark, I thought when I became so independent, so strong, so capable, that I had conquered my mountain. I didn't need anybody. But it was at this point I realized I still had a lot of work to do—a new mountain to climb. I didn't need anyone, but I needed to learn how to want someone.

I didn't just want somebody, though; I wanted him. I wanted Jack back.

It took me another four months to process all of this. To sit back, reflect, write my heart out, realize what I had been doing and how I pushed him away. How I let the love of my life slip by and how it was all my fault. I wrote, and I wrote. I journaled to myself and wrote him letters. Somehow writing something out turns me into my own counsellor, as what I am writing, I read with new eyes. Once it is out on paper – I instantly see. Usually, and up until this instance in my life, writing a letter to someone that never gets sent, gives me relief, except this time it didn't. I wrote in my journal to Jack and left them in a drawer. I wrote letters and ripped them up. I wrote them and burned them – trying to end the energetic cycle.

None of it worked. So instead, I wrote another letter, and I sent it.

That day, and the next, and the next after that, I would hold my breath, my heart would race, and I would start to sweat as I opened my inbox to see if he replied. Days turned into weeks and nothing. Maybe he didn't get it. Perhaps I didn't say things right? I read it repeatedly, critiquing it, and then I realized that although I had reached out I was still playing defence. So I wrote it over and sent another one – literally bearing all. My heart, my soul, my mistakes, my regret. I owned it, and I owned it all.

He still never replied.

It was at this time that I realized how badly I had hurt him. There is not an unkind bone in his body, not one, and the only way he would ever act rudely was if he were deeply hurt. To not even write me back and tell me to fuck off all the way to hell, which I deserved, showed me that I may have done something he would never, ever forget me for. I say forget because what I believe myself is this – we should forgive. We should forgive everyone who has ever hurt or wronged us. Not forgiving someone only hurts us. It only harbours bad energy and resentment and affects our well being. It doesn't mean one iota to the other party that they aren't forgiven. So for the offended, they should forgive, but they should not forget. Forgive the other person and feel peace. But do not forget that they wronged you, and that is how you can protect yourself from them. I hope that he has or will forgive me because although he clearly hasn't forgotten he deserves to live his life in the peace of forgiveness.

Up until this point, this was my Cinderella story playing out. I forgot about the part in the movies where the lovers get torn apart before they end up together forever. It was simply how the story needed to go I told myself, but unfortunately for me, my love-like-the-movies ending was destined to be different.

I have never, ever, heard from him again.

It took a long time for me to accept this, and I'm fully not sure I have. I kept tabs on him through his public Instagram page and cried when I realized he deleted every photo and memory of my existence off his feed. I had mutual friends give me updates on his Facebook and watched from afar as he met someone else, married someone else. There are times I still wish things had been different, but I accept that it is not so, and so to cope, I surrender, send him love, and let him go.

This, my friends, is the other side of manifestation: when it doesn't work out. I did the work, learned my lessons, admitted my wrongs, and tried to manifest him back in my life. But it was not meant to be for whatever reason, and I had to let it go. There's a difference between forgetting and coping though. I think that's the secret with grief. The pain never actually goes away, but we think about it less and develop better skills to cope with it as time goes on. Although I believe a part of me will grieve Jack forever, it was time for me to stop looking backward and direct my energy forward.

I focused on other areas of my life slowly and gradually. I did more hard things. I managed the farm's upkeep, opened a boutique boarding facility, taught equine first aid, became certified in equine-assisted learning. I went to tradeshows, brought in retail products and built up the company I call Prime Equine as my side hustle. I quit my day job working with my dad after 20 years to see if I could make it independently in the corporate world. I became the Executive Director for a national charity; I bought a new horse, and I took up the sport of mounted shooting. I did things that scared me. I pushed my limits of independence and introversion to what I had never thought I could achieve.

I continued to travel alone, hiking mountains and coulees, but I also learned how to travel with others. Taking Jack to Palm Springs had made me feel absolutely invaded. I needed to learn how to share my life with other human beings, but I needed to start slow. That next spring, I spent an epic weekend in Port Angeles, Washington with a group of strangers. I had signed up for the trip through a women's adventure travel group. I travelled to Victoria by plane, then Washington by ferry, just me and my backpack, meeting up one Thursday evening with seven other women I had never met before. I rode a bike for the first time in 20 years to the ocean side. We portaged on a homemade raft on the lake with the locals. I made friends out of strangers, and at the end of the trip, I left the group to spend some travel time alone. I returned to Victoria, BC, signed up for a whale watching tour and got to bear witness to the blowpipes and fin dives of the humpback whale. It ended up being the perfect combination between sharing experiences with others and remaining independent. For my outward highlight reel, I was fearless. I was living my best life. Nothing could drag me down from here. I may have been alone, but I was living the best view – at the peak of my mountain top.

17

2020 VISION

I was on my annual Solo in SoCal trip on March 4, 2020, when the first cases of Covid-19 were reported in Los Angeles, the first reported cases to reach the US. Our family's property is in Palm Springs, just two hours away from LA. I looked myself in the mirror and said yep; it's a good time to go home! I was scheduled to travel just two days later and felt safe that I was long ahead of the virus.

It had been another epic trip to Palm Springs, and I had come so far from my first trip there alone over eight years ago. On my first adventure, I felt like a baby puppy. Tripping over myself and my suitcase, fumbling through the airport, no one to bounce ideas off like what time I should be where for my connection, do I have time to eat, and what direction was E-wing? Landing in Palm Springs for the first time by myself was absolutely liberating. If you have never travelled alone – you need to. Just do it. Go anywhere, and do it alone. You will find your strengths, and you will find your weaknesses. But above all, you will find yourself.

Getting lost is part of the adventure. Doing WHATEVER you want to do, when you want to do it, listening to your intuition and inner voicer, honouring yourself. You can't go to a resort to do this; you have to go somewhere local, grab an AirBNB, rent a car, shop at the local grocery store, google local attractions and choose things that interest you, do them by yourself, meet new cool people, or sit at the pool alone. We are so inundated with other people's thoughts and opinions these days that we can't hear ourselves. At home, I live alone, and I still have trouble hearing myself. Other people are everywhere in our lives. Unplug. Shut the phone off. Yes, we all have responsibilities and need to be available in a realistic manner, but for four hours every morning when I am in California, I am unreachable. I am out in the mountains, hiking, climbing, exploring, taking photos, bird watching, being silent, connecting with all the things mother earth has to offer us. And it is glorious. Those ten days each year recharge me, reconnect me with myself and this universe. I read and do yoga, I journal, sit by the pool, and read some more. I go for walks or a bike ride after supper, and I watch the sun set. I am outside every minute of every day, and then I sleep. I fit in perfectly with the seniors demographic of Palm Springs because I go to bed at 7 pm, and I'm up at 5 am.

Palm Springs gets better every year, but in 2020, my trip had been extra fun. For the last few years, I started to arrive a day or two at the tail end of my parent's trips. Mom and I would go shopping, out for lunch, and dad would work and then we'd sit out on the patio and have supper in the glorious February heat. Then I usually spend the rest of my trip alone, but this year I had a friend join ME for the last few days of my journey. It was like experiencing Palm Springs in an entirely different way. I had grown to the point where sharing Palm Springs was no longer an infringement on my independence. Instead, I felt like a tour guide, taking Laura to my favourite places, sharing the magic of them with her too. Sharing this sacred place wasn't something I was able to do when I took Jack to SoCal. I felt claustrophobic, invaded, suppressed. This wall being broken down must mean I was growing! More lessons checked off the list! On our last day together, we went hiking at a place neither of us had been. It was far down in the Coachella Valley, a pretty good drive from Palm Springs even though you never leave the view of the city.

We had to take a detour through a vineyard to get there, grabbed some fresh California oranges off the vine and hiked one of the most exciting and terrifying hikes I had been on – slot canyons full of rickety old ladders to ascend and descend the canyon. I would never have done that hike by myself. I was learning there is a time for fierce independence and the ability to rely on yourself, but something can be said about shared power and leaning on another person to level up.

I. Was. Killing it. Personal growth I see you, and I raise you everything I've got - I am all in.

I was on top of the world as I arrived back at home. COVID-19 be gone, whatever. I had worked at home for the last 18 months anyway, and the charity I contracted for focused on mental health in agriculture. I felt secure in my employment, and during these times, I knew we would be needed more than ever. I was set up with my home office, had no kids to home school or spouse to share space with, and had enough toilet paper to make it without a restock for months. I was so blessed not to have any job security or financial worry throughout any of COVID-19, which was a tremendous blessing, considering what I was about to go through next.

I began googling "migrated IUD" in March after returning home from California and was horrified by all the potential complications that could come with that. I had been experiencing a significant increase in womanly body fluids since early in the new year. It was the three-year mark of when my IUD needed to come out, so I quickly attributed this symptom to the fact that something was maybe going on with it. Now a few months later, it was getting even worse, but now Covid was in full swing and most medical appointments were being done by telephone. Another easy excuse to put it off a few more weeks until the virus settled down (ha).

Then, I started hemorrhaging blood in the middle of the night. I'm talking waking you up and out of bed, and I would sit over the cold porcelain in the middle of the night, bleeding and waiting for it to stop. I had always had an extremely short and light monthly flow. With my IUD, I barely even had a flow at all over the last three years. Now I knew something was wrong, really wrong, but again I blamed it on the IUD. Reading the symptoms and medical interventions of a migrated IUD sounded terrible, but not a complete match for what I was experiencing. Still, enough to be the reason I called and booked an appointment to get it taken out. Luckily for me, because of Covid and the halt of any non-essential in-person visits, I was able to get in with my doctor just a few days later.

It was during these days I began googling more and more. With symptoms of reproductive organ and female cancer – irregular bleeding came up a lot. Your mind can make up some pretty incredible stories for you to help keep you "safe" during times of stress. In my head, it was still the IUD causing problems, and the surgery for its invasive migration was something I now welcomed being the reason for my symptoms. Especially once I started researching more and more about cervical cancer, learning that it usually presents no signs at all. Once it does start showing symptoms like bleeding and back pain, it was in a more advanced state and survival statistics are not high.

I also read that cervical cancer is very slow growing. This eased my anxiety, and I was able to argue against the advanced stage statistic. I had followed my doctor's orders and had my pap tests done every three years. I had just got another letter in the mail to go for my next recommended swab; I had done it all right. There was no way that it was cancer.

My brain went into total protection mode, and I let it. Usually, I would keep things like this to myself, but as I had been growing, learning, sharing, I reached out and shared with three close gal pals of mine. They were all there with supportive texts and calls, cheering me on the morning I went to my doctor's appointment. "By lunchtime, this will all be over!" was the resounding theme of their support, and for it, I was grateful.

As I sat in the doctor's office, there was a poster for the HPV vaccine on the wall, citing 90% of cervical cancer was caused by a strain of the virus. I remembered asking my doctor about it when I started being sexually active, but she said I was too old and it was given to pre-teens. She was a doctor, my doctor, so I took her advice and left it at that. But I had been struggling with her for the last few years. I rarely have needed medical treatment, and I've had about six prescriptions in my entire adult life. So when I needed her, it meant I needed medical intervention, and she had been making me feel unheard.

When she walked in that day, I described my symptoms to her, and how incredibly abnormal it was and how worried I was. She didn't even look me in the eyes as she brought up my chart on the office computer. "Mmmmm, yes, okay, well, let's get this IUD out, and we can go from there."

Except, she couldn't get it out. She couldn't find the strings for its removal. She barely tried. "I'll have to refer you to a gynecologist. Do you have a preference?" "Uh – who can see me the fastest? This really is concerning me."

"Well, okay, I'll put you in a 'general pool' referral basket, and whoever can see you first, you'll see." *Oh great*, I thought, *one mediocre general practitioner to another mediocre specialist.* With our population boom over the last few decades, even getting a family doctor was a challenge. The best ones were never accepting new patients. At least any gynecologist would have more training than her, and what else was my option.

After one more bout of sharing my extreme concern for my health, she extended me an olive branch. "If it gets worse in the next few weeks, call back, and we will see what we can do about getting you an emergency appointment."

I walked out of the clinic, set the alarm on my phone for 48 hours later, knowing that I would call back then to lie and say it was worse than it had been because, in my heart of hearts, I already knew it was that bad.

I went home and proceeded to bleed profusely after the appointment, literally passing blood clots. It went on for so long, and was so bad, I called the clinic back and demanded to talk to a doctor, any doctor because mine had, of course, gone home. I spoke to the walk-in practitioner who read my clinic notes and pacified my terror by saying, "Well, there is a note here that you had a very friable cervix, which means it is easily irritated so you may bleed more. It should clear up in another few hours, and if not, go to emergency." Oh good. It did clear up as the day went on, but I bled again that night and the night after that.

Two days after my failed IUD removal appointment, I called back to the doctor's office and told her it was worse, much worse, and I needed something to be done now. At least at this point, I had her attention. I felt I should have had it two days ago, but I'd take it now. She took almost two hours getting back to me, stating that no gynecologist could see me, but she persuaded one obstetrician to see me – in an hour.

Thank God. I packed up and left for the city immediately. I arrived early, and since I work from home and don't go to the city often, I hadn't realized the full extent of COVID-19 lockdowns. The clinic doors were locked, and they would not let me in until the doctor was ready to see me. There had been no parking available in the lot next to the clinic, and I had had to park my huge farm truck a few blocks down. It wouldn't do to walk all the way back then run when they called me, so I stood and paced in the frigid spring temperatures until they let me in.

My ultrasound went swimmingly, and the tech assured me the IUD was placed in the exact correct position. I don't remember if I felt relief or dread. They moved me to another room where the obstetrician had better tools and equipment for IUD extraction and would now remove this object from my body so I could get on with my life.

She came in and made small talk, the general kind you need to make before someone you've just met has their hands up your hoo-hoo. I explained my brief history to her and threw in a nervous, "I don't know what's going on unless it's cancer, ha ha ha."

"Oh," she assured me, "I'm sure it's not that. You're far too young and too healthy. You don't smoke, and you're not overweight. You don't have heart issues or diabetes. Let us get you on the table and take a look."

No longer than it took her to say that did she put a scope into my womanly abyss and state. "Oh. There is a mass. Can you lay still like this while I get a biopsy kit? I didn't bring one in."

I breathed when she told me to breathe; I held tight and wiped a small tear from my eye as she completed the procedure. She had me sit up, and while I had a sheet over my legs, I was still spread eagle in the stirrups. I looked down at her sitting on the stool below me, as this woman, someone I had never met before, looked me in the eyes with her big blue eyes, the crinkle at their corner was the only facial expression I could see behind her COVID-19 protection mask, as she told me, "I wouldn't say this unless I were sure. I will still send it away for biopsy, of course, but I am certain that you have cancer."

18

THE FOREST, OR THE TREES

I remember asking her questions, but I didn't remember any of the answers as soon as I left the clinic. I had spent the majority of my career in healthcare navigation and patient advocacy. My brain automatically had asked all the right questions, next steps, expectations, what was my role, who would I hear from next, but I could not retain a word. Cancer. Cancer, Cancer, Cancer - is all I heard.

In an instant, a single moment, the incredible life I was living turned upside down. I had just turned 37 years old six days prior. I was now facing one of the most devastating diseases ravaging humankind. One in every two women and one in every three men will get cancer once in their lifetime. I would have rather lived a hundred other lives before I would choose this one. I had cancer.

A million thoughts began rushing through my mind. *Was I going to die? How did this happen? What the hell? I am healthy, and I am fit. I deal with my emotions, get lots of exercise, and live my best life. Do I need to write a will? What is going to happen to my dogs if I die? Who can I give them to that would take as good of care of them as me? I don't want to die. I'm not ready to die. I have so much more to live for! Will I have to do chemo? Will I lose my hair? I just grew it out! It's just hair, Adelle. This is your life. You need to worry about living before you worry about losing your hair. What am I going to tell people? Am I going to tell people? I don't want to be sick. I had my regular pap screenings. How did it miss this? Why me? What did I do to deserve this?*

These thoughts and more repeated like a broken record in my mind, over and over and over. I stopped at my parents' house, told my family, and then I went home; I wanted to be alone. When things get tough, I've always wanted to be alone. I was grateful I didn't have a partner; I didn't know what I would say or how I would act. I didn't want to be consoled, hugged, touched. I instantly closed up, and the only company I wanted was that of my dogs.

As I had these millions of thoughts running through my mind, I was coherent enough to know I also needed to take action. I would not wait for any doctor or our healthcare system to begin my treatment of healing this disease. I needed to be in control of something during this time that I felt absolutely out of control. Less than four hours after that doctor looked me in the eye and gave me the news that had the potential to ruin my life, if not end it, I was on the phone taking action. By 8 pm that evening, I had a fully regimented cancer-fighting natural supplementation protocol from my good friend and naturopathic clinic owner, where I had been doctoring for the last eight years.

I have been a big believer in integrative medicine after an experience in my late 20s left my conventional doctor and neurologist with their heads scratching: me experiencing symptoms they wanted to call Multiple Sclerosis, but I wasn't medically presenting that way with the diagnostics. My naturopath and a live blood microscopy identified an infestation of parasites in my blood (I have the picture if you don't believe me). These parasites running through my veins were causing my dizziness, ear ringing, and extremity tingling and numbness. I went on an extensive parasite protocol, and my symptoms cleared up in 90 days, never to return.

When this happened, I was floored. My general practitioner was ready to diagnose me with MS anyway and start me on a synthetic drug protocol for it. I would never have got better. I would have gotten sicker and sicker, maybe ended up with actual Multiple Sclerosis. Clearly, my immune system was already on vacation with this parasite infestation. From then on, I went faithfully twice a year to my naturopath, who was dedicated to my health. I'd have a few things here and there, a little candida overload that would flare up acne, sticky red blood cells that would make me tired, increased platelets, all things that I'd take a few natural supplements for a few months and would clear up.

You might be wondering, as I did, how cancer was able to sneak by my dedication to my health. It was one of the first things I asked my friend and clinic owner. Unfortunately, unlike many other common cancers (ovarian, prostate, breast, etc.), there are no tumor markers in blood-work for a few cancers, namely lung, brain, and cervical cancer.

So although I had been active in my caring for myself, it hadn't been good enough.

I was at a tipping point here. I had spent days researching my survival prognosis, something I had no way of knowing because I wasn't staged. I hadn't even had a diagnostic scan. The obstetrician had told me that, visually, it was pretty large. She estimated 2 inches. I remember having my measuring tape out, holding it up to my abdomen and looking at how big 2 inches was. I looked up every staging protocol in the world, looking for one that called this size a stage 1, but it just wasn't the truth. I looked for care standards that said it would be a quick surgery, removing my childbearing organs. I didn't care if I lost them; I never wanted to have kids of my own anyway. Unfortunately, according to every treatment centre globally, surgery was not an option for a tumor that size. Then there was the concern of, what if it had spread? What if I was full of cancer, and this was the beginning of my slow demise?

A little voice inside my head started nagging. I couldn't live here. I couldn't stay here. I needed help, and I needed it now. I immediately shifted my mindset and began a mantra of the belief that beating this disease would be 80% mental and 20% physical. I needed to get in a healing headspace, and the natural supplements alone weren't going to be enough. I believed there was some deep-rooted reason that I got cancer, and I needed to figure it out, fast.

My entire adult life, I have worked with energy, manifestation, affirmation, and it's done some damn cool things. I didn't understand how I could have been so spiritually in tune with my life and miss something as big as cancer developing in my body. There was something here, something profound, and I knew it would kill me if I didn't figure out what it was.

When I began to shift my focus this way, the things I needed to know or hear or learn began appearing to me. That first weekend after being verbally diagnosed, I somehow came across a book called *How To Starve Cancer* by Jane McLelland. She had pioneered her way through her stage IV diagnosis of cervical cancer. Now on the off chance you aren't familiar with cancer, stage IV in western medicine is the road's end. Treatment options are not considered curative. They are considered palliative and intended to extend your time on this earth only, and sometimes, they kill you faster than the cancer can. Well, Jane looked her death sentence in the eye, said challenge accepted, and cured herself with integrative care, nutrition, supplementation, generic off label drugs, and literally starving her cancer. I read her entire book online in one day, going through a rollercoaster of emotion. *If she can do it, I can do it!* I kept reading, it then felt like learning what she knew was insurmountable. I kept reading anyway and then went out the following Monday and bought the physical copy to read again, make notes, and highlight. She was living, thriving, 20 years after being diagnosed with stage IV cancer, the same type of cancer as mine.

Next, I somehow fell upon Louise Hay's meditations for cancer. I've been a big fan of Louise's work for years, but I had never known that she, too, had cervical cancer.

It was not lost on me that these books and recordings were falling into my lap. The universe was providing them to me, allowing me to embrace this journey and learn the lesson it had for me, that my soul had signed up to complete on this earth walk. And, if not - it would very likely kill me. I chose, like all the times before, to strap on my boots and start hiking my next mountain of life.

At first, I didn't understand why cervical cancer. I do believe that disease causes disease. But I didn't have any dis-ease. I loved my life! I was doing all the stuff and things, facing the world head-on. I had nothing to complain about. I was grateful each day, blessed with a great job, a beautiful home, and the love of many animals. I travelled and had great friends. What was so wrong with me that I had got cervical cancer?

I could have lived in this "why me" state. Many do. But I dug, and I searched, and I went deeper. Louise referenced generational trauma, how we are all just victims of victims. I got on the phone with my energy worker Trisha for a distance session immediately. Through a drumming meditation, I saw a girl and a man in black. I saw a tree with a grave, and when she coaxed me to look inside, the grave was full of daisies. When I came out of the meditation, my energy worker said this experience stems from 11 generations back. I wasn't just healing myself; I was ending the trauma of 11 generations of women in my family. We dissected my visualization. I had been afraid of the grave, that it meant it was my own. Trisha said the grave is a gift - that I have a chance to unbury the past and truly release it forever. The daisies she said represent both the sun with its petals, the new moon with its dark centre, and Freia, the Goddess of femininity.

As I meditated more and journaled more, the reason for my illness began to become clear for me. I related my cervical cancer, part of a woman's reproductive organs and power centre of creation, to my disconnection from the feminine. I never wanted kids, not needing or appreciating my childbearing organs, being wildly independent and able to do anything a man can do, calling myself a pretty boy, taking pride in not needing a man - especially after my life with Mark. I realized I was living heavily on the masculinity side of life and had no balance with the feminine. I had completely shut out and even disliked the blessings of being a woman.

And then, on top of all that, there's what happened to little Adelle.

19

HEAR ME NOW

I was sexually assaulted when I was a child.

Up until this point I had rarely, if ever, talked about it. I was too ashamed, and I argued with myself that I was over it, so I didn't need to put it out there in the world. Except I realize now I wasn't over it, and the walls I thought I had built up after the abuse I tolerated from Mark were actually stemming from this instance long before. I had work to do to heal from it if I wanted to heal my body from this cancer.

I don't know how old I was exactly. But I was too young to understand what it was or that it was wrong.

I remember this came to light for me when I was in grade 4, so I'd have been about 8. Our teacher rolled in the big old box TV on its rickety AV cart into the classroom one day at school. Let me tell you, back in the late '80s, this was the indication of a good day in school! Except we didn't watch a fun movie or the Flintstones that day - we watched a film on inappropriate sexual contact.

Wait. What. What was this? Little Adelle thought to herself. But in class, she didn't say much. We had a "reading nook" in our classroom, and for a book nerd like me, it was my favorite place in the school. A little corner walled by books and filled with pillows. My kind of heaven. At recess, I went in there, and I don't remember how the conversation got started, but I remember being quiet and reserved and, upon prompting, saying to my friend Allie, "That happened to me."

"What?"

"The movie we just watched, that happened to me." This was the first time I connected the dots that I had been in that scenario - and that it was wrong. In an effort to console me, we made plans for me to come over after school to play with her dog, which made me feel better.

But sometime between then and class starting back up, she told our teacher what I had admitted to her. Of all things, my teacher removed me from the classroom to wait in the hallway. I stood there shaking, embarrassed. I had never been sent to the hallway, and now what I had said got me in trouble. It was my first brush with shame, at 8 years old. After what seemed like an eternity, she came out of the classroom, and I stood there awkwardly while she demanded to know what I had said, so as tears ran down from my eyes, I explained for the first time to anyone - what had happened to me.

He was a teenager, and I was a kid, no more than 5 or 6. He locked the door to the spare bedroom in the basement of my childhood home. He made me lay on the bed and undress to my underwear. He put a rolled-up towel over my eyes, look inside my underwear, and then rubbed himself on me. I don't remember what he said to appease this behaviour or how long it went on for. My brain has locked it out. All I know is that it went on for long enough that my cousin, his brother, was upset he wasn't included in the group, so he started banging on the door. Then he kicked a hole in the door. That's when the parents upstairs got alerted, and it stopped quicker than it had started.

I don't remember if he told me not to tell or if I just didn't tell. I sure wish we had got caught.

We.

He.

How easy women share the blame of an assault. But we sure got in trouble for not including our cousin in our activities, locking the door, and thereby ruining Dad's beautiful new oak door. I don't think he ever got it fixed—a constant reminder of that day.

So, here I am, replaying this for my teacher, out in the hallway like a bad girl. She left me out in the hallway again after my confession. Presumably, she went to call my mom... but there I sat alone, with more shame for admitting this memory. At one point, someone took me to the nurse's station. It's all a blur. But I remember once I was in the blur, I wanted to be out of it. I wanted to take it back; I didn't like this attention, this separation. I just wanted to play with my friend and her dog.

Somehow, I got home. I'm not sure if I walked, or if my mom came to pick me up because of the circumstance. I don't remember if it was in the middle of the day or after school. I don't know what my mom said to me, if she hugged me, or what.

I remember sitting in the living room, overhearing her talking to... someone. All I remember hearing was, "How can I tell her? She raised her boys right. They go to church, and they are devoutly Catholic. If I tell my sister, she will be devastated."

I remember asking if I could go to Allie's to play with Fred, the poodle. Can I escape from this uncomfortable feeling now, please?

I don't remember what my mom and I talked about, or if we talked about it. What I remember the most about that day, what I remember vividly carrying into my teens, young adulthood, and into my mature adult life – is nothing.

I don't remember ever talking about it again. No one ever told me if they spoke to my aunt or my cousin – if anything had happened, repercussions of his inappropriate actions.

I walked around comatose for years at our family gatherings, skirting my cousin in any way that I could. It was probably more manageable when I was younger, still childlike and carefree, but as I got older, started exploring my sexuality, it got harder to ignore. It began when I was going through my first real relationships—being young and in love, yet lacking confidence, ashamed, and afraid. Boyfriends would get frustrated with me when I would "playfully" push their hands away, say no and giggle. I thought I was being flirty. One boyfriend finally explained to me I was being hurtful. Wow. I connected the dots, and so, I told him. The first person I had told since grade 4.

After that, I would tell my boyfriends but use it as an excuse to avoid extreme intimacy. Be patient with me. Understand where I'm coming from. But all the while, it was me continuing to keep my walls up instead of dealing with my past and healing.

No wonder I got cervical cancer. I did have dis-ease, and it finally caused disease.

I thought I had done my work. I "forgave" him. I "forgave" my mom. But every time I saw him, I refused to speak to him. I figured it was okay to forgive but not forget. I couldn't believe how my mom could talk to him like nothing ever happened. Did they think I lied?

Then, about eight months before I was diagnosed, he tried to friend me on Facebook. Delete. Do you not remember what you did to me? We are friends off, for life. Asshole.

Because this feeling came up for me so hard and fast, I battled with confronting him about our past. Does he even remember? A quick few minutes when we were about 6 and 12... I didn't want to face him. I felt I didn't have to in order to forgive him.

I realized how much work I had to do to heal my cancer, truly. Cervical cancer – the root/sacral chakras. Emotion, emotion, emotion. Love, sexuality, creation, relationships. Femininity. Growth of life. From 6 years old, I have been living disconnected from this area until it finally caused disease. I was chronically in the worst relationships I ever could have been in, dating drug dealers, drug users, alcoholics, narcissists, and gaslighters, and then the universe brought me the most fantastic relationship I ever could have wished for, and because I refused to let down my walls, deal with my issues, my baggage, I burned it down.

It was not just me and my intimate relationships that suffered. When I think back (I've genuinely had this revelation as I am writing this book), it was about grade 4 is when my mom and I started to drift apart. I used to blame it on her for not being the mom I wanted, but looking at it now, maybe it was me who pulled away. Distancing myself in order to protect my inner child when I had not felt protected. We started fighting about clothes, what I would wear, how I would do my hair. By grade 9, I was buying most of my own clothes and necessities with babysitting money. I never really leaned on her. I didn't feel she was the mom I wanted her to be. Going for lunch, shopping, talking about heartbreak and boys, we didn't do these things, and I didn't disclose anything to her at all. I was uninterested in opening up to her about anything in my personal life; a part of me didn't trust her.

As I wrote this, I have always wanted to blame her for not being the mom I wanted. I worked long and hard on accepting my mom for who she was, understanding that my soul had chosen my parents to be my family before I came to earth, and even in the past few years, our relationship has been better. But at this point in my diagnosis, I realized: maybe she had been the mom I needed, and I refused ever to accept it.

With these revelations shaking me to my core… I vehemently wanted to stop using the experience as a crutch, an excuse to be intimately shy and disconnected from the blessings of love in this life. I decided I want to be free. I also realized this was no easy task, and I had so much work to do. I was dedicated to my lesson now. Cancer. It was healing or bust.

I chose life.

Challenge accepted.

20

HOOFPRINTS IN THE SAND

The biopsy confirmed that my doctor was correct; I did indeed have cancer. Adenocarcinoma cervical cancer is a less common cell type and is regularly missed on a pap test. So although I had regular pap smears, I still got cancer. I didn't know how to cope. My parents didn't know how to cope. I didn't know how to talk about it, and I couldn't even say the word out loud. It felt taboo to speak its name, for surely it just couldn't be true. I was only 37 years old. Could they be wrong? I couldn't comprehend the word cancer meshing into my life and was in a spiral about it.

A self-proclaimed control freak, I felt out of control, which made me spiral harder. During times of grief or extreme life circumstances, I have coped by staying busy - but not with the everyday things that usually keep me busy. I couldn't focus on work, so I researched. The first two weeks after my diagnosis while I was waiting for scan dates and doctor's appointments, it was time to start planning my own treatment. Since day one of my presumed diagnosis, I had been religiously taking my naturopathic supplements; and if there were any other alternative treatments I could do, I would. I started by acknowledging that I ate like shit. I ate what I called "balanced." I told myself I ate healthy 80% of the time when, in reality, it was the other way around. I'd binge on a salad for four days in a row so the veggies wouldn't go to waste, then I headed to the cupboards or the freezer for meals over the next week or two until I went back to the grocery store. I grocery shopped like once every 3 weeks - so if that gives you any indication about how fresh my food was... yeah, it was not fresh. This didn't concern me though because I was thin, which meant I had a good metabolism. So why would I eat vegetables every day when I could get away with eating a personal pan pizza?

I was addicted to candy and sugar. As I started my journey of acknowledging my diet and cleaning out crappy foods, I threw out bags and bags of sugary sweet treats in my house. I filled more than one kitchen garbage bag full. Part of me wishes I had kept eating those treats for a few days and counted the grams of added sugar I consumed in a 24-hour period, I expect it would be astronomically high.

I would eat bags of sour patch kids like an alcoholic would down two bottles of wine. No. Big. Deal. When I was in my 20s, I ate candy AND drank a 500 ml bottle of soda every day after lunch. I couldn't get through the afternoon without it. After I turned 30, I cut the soda and lost 5 pounds I didn't think I had to lose.

So, from my 20s to my 30s, I made progress by cutting the cola. I was winning. Except I was fueling my cancer. I don't know when it started to grow, but since cervical cancer is a slow-growing cancer, I am sure I had been spoon-feeding it for years. When we consume sugar, the body produces insulin. Insulin secretion governs the accretion of our physical growth, and as adults, now that we are done growing, we don't need to grow anymore. The bad part about insulin overreacting to us dumping copious amounts of starch and sugar in our body is that insulin tells our body to grow. Since there's no record of adults getting any taller, the research suggests it tells other things, like the cancer seeds that live inside us all to grow.

Thanks to my research on how to starve my cancer, I transformed my kitchen overnight. I threw out garbage bags of snack foods and freezer meals and was suddenly on a no refined sugar, low carb, low saturated fat, no dairy, low glycemic, whole food diet. Bam.

I do not recommend it.

Well, technically, I do recommend it, but not doing it overnight. I was scared shitless that I was going to die, so I needed that kick in the ass to get me rolling down a new diet track. I genuinely don't know if I would have done things differently, but in my work now, my goal is to encourage other people to change their lives BEFORE they get cancer or disease, so if that is you – I suggest going slowly. I really should have known better. As an equine nutrition consultant, the number one rule of making feed changes for horses is to do it slowly so as not to disrupt the sensitive microflora in the animal's guts, which causes inflammation, blockages, and extreme discomfort. The same goes for any dog-owners. Make changes slowly and over a few weeks to the new diet. I always make sure to follow those rules for my pets. But for me? Nope change all the things- today!

I was eating the cleanest I ever had in my entire life combined... and I had a basketball living in my torso. Overall, I felt terrific. I had tons of energy and was working out. I was healthy, fit, lean, and in a great mind space, but I was constantly bloated, which actually lasted for about four months. But learning and mastering a new diet was a distraction, and one I needed badly. It was something different to focus on: learning how to cook, count carbs, understand caloric intake, and researching low glycemic foods.

Being in control of things like my diet gave me a sense of peace. I struggled through my entire treatment and diagnosis with seeing other people. How could I be around normal people when I was wandering around every minute of every day wondering if I was going to die? Working in mental health, I understood that I needed to let myself "feel the feel," to not shove the grief, sadness, disbelief, disappointment, and shame under the rug. I battled shame immensely when I would be out in a social setting. My parents had told a few of their close friends, for they needed support going though this too. I was okay with that, but when I would see them, I felt this immense cloud of darkness in the room, an unspoken secret, fueling my shame. I didn't want to talk about it, acknowledge it, let alone wonder what other people thought about the girl who got cancer.

Shame is a dark feeling, and I wish it on no one, even though it is already engrained deeply in most of us. I was ashamed all the time: of myself, of being sick, of not being strong, of needing help. I retreated more inward than I ever have before. In the period following my diagnosis, I was alone all the time. I even pushed away the things that meant the most to me – my horses. Each day I would go out to check on them, and as soon as I saw them, I would break down in the middle of the field and sob. These creatures that had always been my therapists, my outlet, my relief, my recharge - I was afraid to get close to them in case I died or could never ride them again. And I did what I had always then done once again – run. Push them away. Push people away. To stay in the safety of my fortress. Nothing external could hurt me if I was already isolated and alone.

But as the weeks passed, I grew. I knew that this disease had come to me because of internal dis-ease. If I wanted to survive and thrive, I needed to learn. I needed to break open and to let the light in. So one day, I got back on my horse Ticket, and we rode. We rode, and we rode. The next day after that, we rode again. I let down my guard, and I let her carry me. For a few hours each day, I asked her to take me away, far away from this nightmare that was now my reality. And she did. We logged more miles down the trail in the six weeks leading up to my treatment than I ever have in my life riding horses. I needed support, and I didn't even realize how much. She was helping me break down a deeply seeded wall of isolation, of protection, where instead of me going inward and trusting only myself, I broke open. I allowed another being to be there for me, day after day. As I look back on the memory of those weeks, I realize they were a perfect example where two footprints in the sand during a time of darkness become one.

The last time I was in a hospital was when I was born. Now it felt like I was in the hospital every day. As my treatment planning went on, I went from scan to scan, hospital to hospital – sometimes two different hospitals on the same day. I stared in awe down at my wrist at my admissions band, something I hadn't worn since I was three days old, leaving the hospital in my parent's hometown. I know I have been blessed, so blessed, with health up until this point. No broken bones, no surgery, never anything more than a sniffle or a bout of strep throat. Now here I was, going from zero to 60 overnight. I guess that fits with my lifelong preference for significant change, hey? Looking at it that way though, maybe it is how I needed it to happen to ensure I actually did make a big change in my life because I likely wouldn't have made the shift under any other circumstance.

It was May 2020, full lockdown across the globe due to Covid19. The hospitals felt like prisons. They were silent, desolate, eerie. I was allowed no support person at any of my appointments. MRI's, CT scans, PET scans, I had to get dropped off at the door and picked up after it was over. I ended up in the emergency room after one appointment because I had lost so much blood after a physical exam. I nearly collapsed out in the yard and am so grateful my parents happened to be over that day. Earlier in the afternoon, I had to call them and break down, asking for help feeding the horses because my tumor wouldn't stop bleeding, and I was passing blood clots every time I stood up. I wasn't able to yell or wave for their attention. I crawled into my truck that was nearby and just leaned on the horn until someone came.

My mom wheeled me into the ER, where they promptly turned her away. What? I was in the emergency room due to blood loss, possibly needing a transfusion, and I had never been in the emergency room before as a patient. We were offered zero leniencies, and I spent the entire evening alone in the hospital bleeding out, diagnosed with cancer, and a draining cell phone battery, all by myself.

My fierce independence was lending me strength, but my heart bled for the other patients going through illness. Every time I would go to an appointment at the cancer centre, there would be other people there alone too. Since no one was allowed to accompany a patient into the clinic, it was obvious that everyone in the radiation department had cancer too. I would lower my eyes to the floor and hide behind the shield of my hat when I would see a small, frail grandpa sitting all alone, or another woman, my age, waiting to be treated for cancer. All going through the same thing, but from our six foot distances due to Covid, we couldn't even pass the time by sitting together and talking. This led to even more feelings of shame, just like when I was a little girl waiting out in the hallway for talking about being assaulted. The upward path towards survival was getting harder and harder to climb.

21

SICK CARE

Cancer treatment is known for providing what is called The Standard of Care.

Standard (adj): Used or accepted as normal or average.

Standard? Who wants standard? This was my life we were talking about and I wanted exceptional.

As I was going through treatment, there would be, time and again, instance after instance where I would call my mom or my dad absolutely baffled and bewildered about what was going on with my care. From the outside looking in, I had long believed that our medical system is most definitely behind the times. Now going through it myself, I was convinced of it. At 37 years old, with a 90% survival prognosis, the only option I was being offered was just your average accepted treatment, treatment that came with a myriad of high-risk, long-term side effects.

My treatment options – well, there were no options. According to the Standard, it was chemoradiation or bust. I wasn't sure about the chemotherapy part. I've never been a big believer in healing with poison, and as I sat in front of my oncologists for the first time, I was armed. I had

Jane's *How to Starve Cancer* book. I had Chris Wark's *Chris Beat Cancer* book and his 20 questions to ask your oncologist. I had staging documents from Canada, the USA, and abroad. I had lists of side effects, second and third opinions from medical doctors in other countries, and I was determined to get the best and most individualized care possible, only to find out that the best, most individualized care is not an option in Canada. Let me tell you – free healthcare, definitely comes at a price.

My prescribed plan was for 25 daily external pelvic radiation treatments accompanied by weekly "baby doses" of chemotherapy – promised to be so low of a dose I would have zero side effects from it. After those five weeks of treatment, I would have another four internal radiation treatments spread over two weeks. This protocol was right out of some book, the same plan that anyone else in Canada would be given who was at the same stage as me. How special I felt.

So me being me, I began to earn my honorary doctorate in oncology and started Googling the side effects of radiation, especially pelvic radiation.

Short term side effects I wasn't concerned with. Bladder intolerance, upset bowels, I knew how regenerative our body could be with soft tissue, so I felt comfortable that my holistic approach to my treatment would take care of helping my body restore itself. Five weeks of rushing to the bathroom was a meagre sacrifice for curing cancer.

Long term, that's what started to scare me. Pelvic radiation gave me a 100% chance of going into early menopause, which meant hormone replacement therapy for the rest of my young adult life. Thirteen years ahead of when I would experience nature's menopause, thirteen years of pushing synthetic compounds into my body to replace my non-functioning ovaries. Oral hormone replacement in the past had contributed to a myriad of complications in my life, including bouts of aura and debilitating migraines. Not to mention the fact that it's not recommended for women to be on birth control after 35 as the risk of stroke increases tenfold, and as well would increase my chances of breast cancer. How comforting.

But, okay. I didn't love any of this, but these risks versus not treating my cancer at all… I decided I could handle it and promised myself I would also find a long-term natural solution for replacing those hormones. Many times, I did wish I had a will as strong as Louise Hay, who received no conventional treatment and healed her cancer herself. I thought about it but doubt and fear took over. Maybe she had been a stage 0. I was stage 2. I imagined shrinking the two-inch mass in my body with food and my mind, and I simply didn't trust myself enough. So I decided to accept the risk of side effects and change my tune to what I can control, which is believing I will not have a stroke in the future and looking at the positive – no more monthly visitor!

Lifelong side effect #1 – accepted.

The one side effect I had a real issue with was the risk of pelvic fracture and osteoporosis. A 40% chance, according to my research. A statistic that high is nowhere close to being considered a minor threat (less than 1%). That type of percentage is thereby viewed in the "common and expected" category.

I challenged my doctors about the so-called "Standard of Care." The average age of a cervical cancer diagnosis is 50, which the "Standard" protocol for treatment was based around. I, however, was only 37 years old. I lived on a ranch by myself, ran a boarding facility, fed horses, did repairs, operated the tractor, pitch bales, you name it. I was good day labor. I rode horses, and not just wandering down the trail. In the sport of mounted shooting, we race as fast as we can, wielding two single action revolvers, shooting targets. Riding horses is also my therapy, my reprieve, my happy place, my connection, how I recharge, my every-thing. And for the rest of my life, I would have a 40% chance of busting a hip just jumping off the last step of the tractor?

Ring the alarm. I was not okay with this. I had already spoken with doctors in other parts of the world, where Canada's "Standard of Care" is archaic. You're 37? Twenty-five external radiation treatments? No way, they said. We would give you 10, shrink the tumor then take the organ out entirely. This sounded brilliant, and it was exactly what I wanted (if you have to want for a critical illness treatment plan). To receive this treatment, I would just have to travel halfway around the world and - oh, wait. We're in the middle of Covid-19 and a global lockdown.

I couldn't leave my country to get better medical care, even if I wanted to pay for it out of pocket myself.

I could risk waiting until it was safer to travel… but even as I am writing this book, we are ten months into C-19, and there's no end in sight. I've been done with treatment for months already. I may have a lifelong risk of fractures, but I'm also not sure my mental health could have withstood waiting it out and trying to keep the image of a tumor growing in my abdomen every day at bay.

So I made a choice, the only option. Treatment begrudgingly accepted.

But I challenged the choice– I went the mile in advocating and asking. I would leave no stone unturned in the name of prevention. Could we run a diagnostic MRI halfway through? And if the tumor was gone by then – I could quit?

I technically could quit at any time as I did have free will, but the doctors would never consider recommending that. Edit: they would never be allowed to consider that even if they believed it. You see, it's not my individual doctor's fault. It's because their hands are tied in red tape by the governing board of the national standard. The more I knew, the more I realized… even in a first world country, we aren't really that free.

I voiced my concerns to her. If I do end up being cancer-free – but I have debilitating hip and pelvic osteoporosis and I can't live and manage my farm, ride my horses – quite frankly, that's not a quality of life that would end up well for my mental health. If I'm going to survive, I want to go on for the next 50 years, and I want all of them to be on my farm.

Our compromise after me advocating my ear off? She would request a bone scan before we started treatment.

A COMPROMISE? How is THAT not a standard of care for this high-risk side effect?

She agreed to send me for a bone scan and assured me that changes would not be seen from the radiation for three or more years. This was weird because the report I read and sent to her, that she had also read and agreed with, said that 40% of pelvic radiation patients experienced a pelvic fracture in the first year following treatment.

What's up, doc?

So, I went for the scan, and my bones looked great. I was relieved to at least have a baseline.

I followed up with her yet again, asking, can I do **anything** to help prevent future issues? "Oh no," she said, "but if you start to have osteoporosis – there are excellent drugs we have to slow it down."

Slow it down. React. Not prevent. Herein shines our sick care system and reactive treatment again.

Not satisfied, I pressed harder. "Uhmm, what about taking calcium and magnesium, D3 and K2 supplements?

"Oh, sure," she said. "Yes, those are important nutrients that will help support your bone strength."

I was blown away. *WHY DID I HAVE TO ASK?* And what about all the other patients who don't know how to ask? Patients who put the fate of their lives in their doctors and do whatever and only what they say? I quickly saw firsthand how our healthcare system supports people just getting sicker and sicker their whole lives. I knew I would eventually have to speak out on this, which is what you are reading now.

Still not satisfied with my prescription of a few common vitamins and minerals and continuing my search for ways to make my treatment exceptional, I had an appointment booked with my naturopath for the week after completing my seven weeks of conventional medicine. This is the same clinic I attended who did my first blood microscopy that uncovered the root cause of my misdiagnosed Multiple Sclerosis symptoms as a blood parasite.

So, I went for the follow up with my naturopath, and low and behold, my dried blood microscopy already showed issues of integrity reduction with the bone health in my pelvic region.

Traditional healthcare – a bone scan - would not have shown these changes for maybe another two years, which would have been too late to prevent anything, and these two years of proactive treatment may just be the difference between me living on this farm for 50 years or in an accessible condominium.

In many other countries, they are lightyears ahead of North American healthcare. In a handful of places, they have moved into a "Personalized Oncology" approach. They consider the entire individual human, where they are in life and where they want to be, to thrive (not just survive) and blend conventional with complementary treatments into fully integrative oncology. Mistletoe therapy, an all-natural immunotherapy treatment, is used regularly with cancer patients in Germany. IV Vitamin C is customarily prescribed alongside chemotherapy in Mexico and many other places.

The US is slowly starting to latch on to these ideas, but only in privately funded clinics. Big Pharma has no interest in mistletoe and vitamin C since they are naturally occurring substances and they can't be patented. They would instead take this research and create a synthetic version of these properties so they can be patented, AKA making a profit on.

I could go on and on about this topic, but that's a story for another book. For me and where I was at in my journey, all I knew was this: the standard was not good enough.

22

FRIEND, OR FOE

I could feel my palate change as the poison crept through my veins. Before my treatment started, I spent hours visualizing chemo as healing medicine. Bright white light coursing through my veins, doing no harm. I meditated on it. I journaled on it. The energy worker on my inner circle cancer team helped me focus on it as healing and health.

As I sipped the final sip of my sugar-free almond cream matcha latte from my brand-new ceramic travel mug bought explicitly for my chemo days that read, "let that shit go," I could feel it. I thought I imagined it, that I was making it up. I know the mind can play insane tricks with us. But it crept in slowly. It tasted like metal and felt like a sharp pang. The taste slowly coursed over my tongue and at that moment, during my first dose of chemotherapy, everything changed. After that day, not only could I not stomach the sheer thought of coffee, matcha, mushrooms, or salmon, all items that, 24 hours before, had each been a staple in my diet, but also – I couldn't get out of bed.

I loved my oncologists from the moment I met them, one with spiky blue hair and cool shoes and the other a beautiful girl next door type. Neither of them looked a day over 40. I couldn't believe they were oncologists, and I loved them for breaking the norm. To this day I could imagine us being good friends.

They promised me I wouldn't even feel it. A "baby dose," my medical oncologist called it. It was five tiny little radio-sensitizing doses of chemo once per week to help the radiation do a better job. They considered it 10% of my treatment and the radiation 90%. I would not lose my hair, and I would have no side effects at all. I remembered back to the day sitting in the doctor's office, staring at their masked faces. 90% survival, I heard, surgery is not an option I heard, chemoradiation... my heart dropped. I don't remember a lot of that 2.5-hour meeting, but I remember my hand trailing up to my waist-long locks, petting them, asking them if I would lose it all. They assured me that, no, I would not. As petty as it was, a weight was lifted off my shoulders. I would get treated for cancer and didn't have to lose my hair. I thought chemo was the staple for almost any cancer treatment, and I didn't know the use and frequency of radiation. If I were going to have cancer treatment, God bless me, this is the kind I'd like to have.

I didn't sign the consent for chemo that day, though. I needed to think about it. And by think about it, I mean, my intuition was screaming at me, *no!* But my brain was alerting me to danger, bringing up fear and doubt about not accepting my diagnosis. As I sat signing the radiation form, I recall my dad urgently asking, "Why can't you sign them all?" I understood the fear in his voice, but I was surprised by his force in suggesting I sign up for receiving poison. With the both of us having worked in healthcare for the last 20 and 40 years, we knew and advocated on the importance of individual consent, the ability to understand, and the power to choose. It was not only a personal right, but due diligence. However on this day, the day I was receiving my test results, my cancer staging, and recommended treatments, I was done making decisions and hearing options. I am grateful for my medical oncologist, who pacified this moment of disconnect and understood my saturation point. I had heard enough. She smiled and tucked the form in my hand and said, "Absolutely, there is no rush. Take it, read it, think about it."

They told me chemo had an "average" improvement rating for the treatment of 8-12% towards my overall cure rate. I can't imagine having me as a patient; I questioned everything my doctors told me. I was kind, but I was thorough. And my brain quickly broke down the fact that an "average" rate of 8-12% meant that some people experienced 0% and others 20%. I asked the doctor if I was correct. "Well, yes," she said. For some people, it helped a lot, and for others, it didn't help at all.

I fell into fear. I signed the form, and I never felt good about it. I did my best to rally that day, walking into the chemo department alone. Due to COVID-19 no one was allowed to support me through the five-hour treatment. Since no one could accompany me, and since I would have no side effects, I had also drove myself, not wanting to inconvenience anyone. I had my backpack stuffed full of healthy snacks, a matcha latte, had put on my makeup, wore my new hat, and snapchatted my friends and family, "I've got this!"

I had that one treatment, one dose, and I knew I would never come back for it again, even if it reduced my survival rate by 20%. Chemo undid the six weeks of everything I had worked towards in a single day: the diet, the nutrition, the exercise, my plans. I had visualized that radiation was not going to slow me down, and if chemo wasn't going to give me any side effects, why not take the chance that I might be one of the ones it would help? I would ride horses, sit on the deck, work, and keep on with my regular everyday life. But my gut kept telling me, no, no, no, don't sign the chemo form and I ignored it.

I fell for it, the peer pressure – from my doctors, from my family. No one "said" anything per se, but I could see it in their eyes. Your loved ones, rightfully so, want you to do EVERYTHING available to you and said to you by a doctor, and it is hard to disappoint them. So I said yes. And instead of helping my healing and maximizing my radiation, my one "baby dose" of chemo left me bedridden for six weeks.

It took a few days for it to hit me fully. It started with vertigo. I felt a little bit dizzy, but I kept driving myself to radiation treatments – I didn't want to burden anyone. But the dizziness got worse as each hour went on. My appetite shrunk and shrunk, and by day three, I admitted to myself I could not drive anymore. It took one more day for me not to be able to get out of bed. Extreme vertigo, exhaustion… I've never experienced fatigue like that. Lifeless. It felt like one of those dreams where danger is coming, and you need to run or walk somewhere, but you can only move at a snail's pace. That's what the exhaustion felt like. Some days I would crawl to the kitchen and pry myself up onto the countertop to get yet another snack. I was on four different anti-nausea medications after the chemo but didn't feel nauseous at all. I also had no appetite, but I was hungry every half hour. I was trickle feeding and surely would have starved to death after another four doses of chemo.

I couldn't figure out why I was so hungry all the time but could only eat a few bites before I felt full. I had asked the spry young pharmacist who gave me a baggie full of medication: "What are the side effects of these pills I'm taking to prevent the side effects of chemotherapy, of which my doctor said I wouldn't have any anyway?"

"Oh, none, ma'am."

Except after about five days of trickle-feeding myself to death, I was finally like, OKAY, WHY. And I was ticked off enough to gather some energy to start Googling all the medications I was on. It turns out one of them helps curb your nausea by rapidly increasing the rate at which your stomach digests food, which means you feel hungry faster. This information frustrated me to no end. I was my best advocate and asked all the right questions, and I still couldn't get a straight answer from these medically trained professionals.

I thought it was going to last forever. I felt like I would never get better. I called my doctor on the emergency line two Sundays after my first and last round of chemo. They had abated me and agreed that I was so sick I shouldn't attempt to do week two chemo. I already knew I'd never go back, but I was agreeable and nodded at their recommendation to continue chemotherapy in week three in an attempt to appear amicable. When they finally patched me through to her, I burst into tears and asked if I would be this way for life. There was no reprieve after 11 days, none. Not a flicker of light down a pitch-black hallway. I had been poisoned.

Before I agreed to start the chemo, I had been doing more international research, looking at different options. I asked my doctors about chemosensitivity testing. The testing that is available to anyone in the world, where with a few quick vials of blood drawn, you can have the DNA of you and your cancer cells sent away to a lab where they test each and every chemo drug available against your body for both effectiveness on killing the cancer cells and your personal genome reaction to the side effects of the drug.

Did you know?

I cannot believe this is not mainstream medicine. My doctors did indeed know about it but said that they don't mention it because many patients can't afford it. It is between three and six thousand dollars. Take my advice – if you ever have to go through cancer where chemotherapy is your recommended treatment - take out a loan and get this test. It's worth it. Many stories are out there of patients whose chemo has hastened their death and others where chemo has cured them with barely any side effects. Going through this conversation with my doctor, knowing they don't think to much as mention this to anyone… I can't help but question. If those who suffer under the medicine of what they are praying to cure them had this testing done and could see the results before pouring the drug into their body… I wonder. At the least, I believe we should have the informed right to choose.

I had the testing done. Not only does it test for chemosensitivity, but it also maps out the genome of your cancer and its metabolic pathways. There are many ways to kill cancer, as I had learned by reading books like *Starving Cancer, Radical Remission* and the like. You can make guesses and get consensus from a lot of other research and data, but this cancer testing can tell you precisely what metabolic pathways your cancer feeds off of. So you stop eating the foods that feed it, start eating the foods that nourish your body, take both off-label drugs (medications that are off-patent and therefore there is no significant profit on) and natural supplements that block the pathways from your cancer cells accessing food and... they die. I believe this is the way of future cancer care.

But first, we have to get past this nonsense of treating people with chemo, especially without doing chemosensitivity testing first. Why would the North American drug administrations and the Standard of Care not include chemosensitivity testing in their protocols? Well, cancer treatment and cancer research is a billion-dollar industry. Yet, the five main chemotherapy drugs used were invented and patented in the 1960s. It's 2020. There has been no improvement in chemotherapy drugs or their effectiveness in over 60 years, yet they continue to be the leading treatment plans in cancer patients.

I knew I wanted to get the testing done, even if it was to prove something to myself, my gut instinct maybe. The upside to having cancer during COVID-19 was that my timeline from diagnosis to treatment was rapid since all non-urgent care was on hold. The downside to having cancer during COVID-19 is that I wouldn't have the results back until I was four cycles into my prescribed five chemo cycles. I decided to do it anyway, for if I had a future recurrence, I would know if I was a patient that chemo helped or hindered.

The results from my reaction to the chemotherapy drug they put me on were indeed heightened. This meant that on TOP of the standard and expected side effects of chemo, my genes were even more sensitive to the drug they prescribed for me, meaning I would suffer even more severe side effects than usual. In addition, its effectiveness on my tumor cell death was only 42%. That's not good enough for me to feel as sick as

I did. I can honestly say that if heaven forbid I ever get cancer again, I will not do chemotherapy.

It is such a simple test. That would give people the power to choose whether they wanted to risk being so sick for a 42% chance or if they wanted to choose quality of life for the next however long they had left on this earth. We should be given the knowledge and the power to choose.

I sit here today writing this chapter, sipping my first cup of coffee exactly four months post-chemo. I haven't written about my cancer yet, until today. It's been too fresh, too hard. So I worked on the chapters from my past. But that bitter bite of delicious coffee that finally didn't revolt my senses, I attribute just ever so slightly to another milestone in my recovery. It's been so long since I've had coffee, I don't even really need it. But there's just something about that first sip of coffee in the morning that hits your soul... I have actually grown to be incredibly sensitive to caffeine since I changed my diet, so it's not about the caffeine perk up for me. It's about the fact I've taken that power and my health back - even if I'm drinking decaf.

23

INTO THE DEEP

The cloud came, slowly, strong and dark. It was about week five of my treatment, and I had spent four weeks in bed, napping and Netflixing. I consumed all my meals in my room. I got up to go to the bathroom and started craving going back to bed. My mom did the dishes, my house cleaner cleaned around me, and friends would bring me food. I'd be chauffeured in and out of the city for my treatment, which was a massive 90-minute outing each day, and then head back to bed. My mom and I would cheer on Fridays, that now I had two days off.

In the beginning, I tried harder to rally. *Move the TV out of the bedroom, Adelle. Get your body to at least two different places in your home each day.* Cheer, cheer! But I didn't have the energy or willpower. It was way easier to lay in bed, clicking the tv on and off in between naps. I really liked it when I'd pause a show with intentions to close my eyes for five minutes, and I'd wake up two hours later, and when Netflix goes to sleep, it then rolls through the up and coming show previews. I'd lay there after I woke up and watch them scroll by, making notes in my phone about what show to binge on next.

The urge to move the TV out of the bedroom passed. I began to have thoughts of how awesome this was. I questioned how I would ever go back to work. Laying in bed and watching TV all day was AMAZING. Those thoughts crossed my mind. It became my new normal, and I quickly couldn't imagine it being any other way.

In the beginning, even as sick as I was, I somehow magically forced myself to go outside and feed my horses their grain. It is usually a 10-minute chore, but it took me several minutes alone just to get to the barn. I would almost crawl. I walked hunchbacked, shuffling my feet, determined not to let cancer treatment get the best of me. This wasn't how I planned for it to go. For a while, the horses were my lifeline, my responsibility.

But soon, even the will to go see the horses waned. They didn't really "need" to be fed their mash. I would lay in bed and wait to see if one of the boarders was coming out and offer to do chores for me, letting me know everyone was alive. On the days no one came, I would convince myself their mash was not necessary for life. Dear horses, see you tomorrow. Or the next day. I was convinced that I was rewarding myself by staying inside all day. Responsibility – what 'dat.

There came the point one day when I was lying in bed, and I felt the cloud creep in. I remember it vividly. I was lying like a ragdoll in my king size bed, my obedient and loyal dogs sleeping soundly beside me. Another day with no exercise unless they went and walked themselves. I was spread out like a starfish, head propped up on a few pillows in a haphazard attempt to be a little higher than supine, staring out the window.

Do I care anymore? I asked myself.

I didn't. I didn't care. I don't think I could. I had lived a good 37 years, with more enlightenment, lessons, good times, and experiences than some people dream of. It had been a good shift. If this disease wanted to take me, then fine. I was at the point that I accepted it. Looking back, I think it was my body and brain going into protection mode. It was inducing me into a survival state just to get me through the end of treatment. I didn't care about being grateful, and I didn't care about my diet. I didn't care that I wasn't intermittent fasting. I hated the text messages that would come in, asking how I was doing that day. Who gives a shit.

As I laid there that one particular day, looking out the window, I said to myself, this is depression. This is what it feels like. I could feel it easing a heavy fog through my brain like an early fall morning. I hadn't experienced depression before, so really I wasn't sure, but I had certainly never felt this way in my entire life. I waved my hand through that fog, breaking up its steady path. *Are you depression?* I asked it.

It did not answer.

The small twinkling of what was my normal self started asking: *are you really this sick, or are you being lazy?* I wasn't sure. I couldn't answer. Maybe it was both? After weeks of unrelenting illness and the lack of desire to live, I started to wonder if I was sick sick. Was I the same sick, or better sick, or worse, sick... or succumbing to depression? So many thoughts to think. What was I going to watch next on Netflix?

I let myself be sick. Or depressed. Or both. I just let it. I knew my road might be more challenging when I needed to climb out the other side, but at this point, I couldn't care. Dying didn't seem so bad. At the onset of all this, the pain of the thought of dying would paralyze me in my tracks, drop me to my knees and weep with the rage of a waterfall. But now, hey I am 37. Not everyone gets to live that long. And I've lived a hell of a life, more than some live in 80.

I didn't talk to anyone about it. I had a counselling session booked for my second week of treatment, but I was so sick by then that I couldn't even speak to her, and as the days passed, I no longer cared to. Amidst all the hard things Covid brought, one of the things I was grateful for was that I didn't have a ton of FOMO. I was supposed to be spending the summer traveling the countryside competing in my first year of mounted shooting. I had trained my horse, bought my single-action revolvers, upgraded my trailer; by February, I had been ready. As I scrolled through social media, I'd think to myself, "At least no one else is having any fun either." Even with that, it was hard to look at social media: joy and fun and highlight reels. Looking at profiles of people around my age, healthy, happy, in love, I couldn't help myself some days from asking why they don't have cancer. Why is it me?

I was depressed, but I would scorn myself when those thoughts ran through my head. *How dare I think such thoughts. No one should have to go through this horrible disease, but you are and it's your story, so you get to learn from it or let it kill you.* I knew deep down it was my cross to bear but being so sick through treatment, after I had done so much work to embrace my past, change my life, my diet, my outlook, it was devastating to tumble further down from the mountain top into yet another dark valley.

As I finished external radiation treatments, the worst two weeks were left to come. I only had to go to the cancer centre twice a week, but it was for internal radiation treatments. Although I have never had children, I can confidently say that I can relate to childbirth, without the benefit of nature's hormones dilating my cervix for assistance. Four times. They were long and gruelling days. I had to be there by 8 am, which was a feat since I wasn't waking up until at least 9. I would crawl into my mom's truck, pull my hat low, and we would drive there in silence. They pumped me full of anti-nausea and pain meds to drug me since I would not be able to move, let alone rise off the hospital bed for the next four hours. In the first few treatments, I tried to be a hero and reduce the drugs; I hated how they made me feel. I would go home from treatment after lunch and pass out hard for the rest of the day as well as the day after that. I would feel hungover on top of being sick.

Every conventional form of medication I had throughout my treatment gave me extreme side effects: the anti-nausea meds from the chemo and the chemo itself. I spent half a day with a paralyzed bladder due to the sedation for the surgery to implant my brachytherapy sleeve. These pain meds for radiation were no different. I was growing to hate synthetic pharmaceuticals more than I ever had before. But by the last day of brachytherapy, I couldn't even care anymore. I was done, depressed, exhausted. I had no more fight, no more try. I was in full-on survival mode as I asked them to pump as many drugs as they could into my body so I could sleep through the treatment and try to forget it all ever happened.

24

IT'S OVER NOW

"Yahoo!"

"Hooray!"

"You did it!"

"It's all up from here!"

Excuse me? No.

Well-intentioned words of encouragement from my friends and family streamed through my phone and messages as I finished treatment. Except, the end of my treatment left an extremely anti-climactic feeling inside of me. I was grateful to be done, but I was far from elated. I knew everyone meant well, and I was truly happy and thankful for their support. But every time someone cheered me on and my excitement just couldn't match theirs, I realized it was because I was thinking:

What if I die.

What if I still die?

For a cancer patient, being done with treatment doesn't equate to being done with having cancer. It never will. It's like how an alcoholic will always be a recovering alcoholic. My cancer could always come back, and I will be in remission for the rest of my life. I fought myself on these feelings and emotions, challenging myself, asking if this was me hanging on to depression with my pessimistic outlook or if it was my truth.

Cancer was far from over for me once my treatment was done. Treatment is treatment; that didn't mean it would be successful. Many cancers come back, and you probably know someone who that has happened to, if not yourself. I had follow-up scans booked for three months from the end of treatment that, if they came back clear, simply meant I had extended my leash on life. My leash was already short and included never straying too far from my diet, my exercise, my journal, and my inner child - to keep up and keep ahead of allowing these poisonous cells to conglomerate and create illness in my body again.

If you ever find yourself supporting someone with cancer, my words of advice are this: instead of being a positivity cheerleader, ask. Ask them how they are finding this process. Do they need a cheerleader, or do they need a tissue? For all you know, someone could be grieving being done treatment. If they aren't in a place to take radical control like I was, they may be desperately worrying if their treatment was enough to cure them and living in fear that it wasn't now that they aren't getting anymore. Some people don't have the capacity to take on the task of belief and manifestation, exercise and supplements and a healthy diet - to throw out all the stops at cancer as I did. Being done with treatment could be scaring the shit out of them. For me, in my situation, I would have rather celebrated being finished treatment as a milestone, not as the end. That resonated with me. It was a huge, everloving milestone on this journey with cancer... that will never be over.

I've come to peace with the fact. As I live my life, I will always be looking over my shoulder to see if cancer is lurking in the shadows. I won't let it consume my life, but I will use that to fiercely protect and remind myself to continue exercising, eating healthy, getting my mind right, and healing my emotional wounds. Cancer scared me straight, and it will always be a part of my story.

I don't know. Maybe I'm the crazy one. I'm usually the black sheep anyway. If so, how do other people do it? Do they do it? Do they just get cancer, get treatment, resume daily pre-cancer life and never think about it again? Is that a thing? For me, it was a wake-up call, a radical lifestyle shift, a midlife crisis. I can only pray that, at 37, this is just the beginning of my mid-life phase.

It was getting to the point where I was getting miffed every time someone would cheer me on for being done treatment. As much as I do still believe people should heed my advice on permissions-based conversations with their loved ones going through treatment for a life-threatening illness, to those who are sick – this part is for you. To realize it's not at all about the other person; it's about you. When what someone else is "doing" pisses you off, it's time to go inward, feel this feeling, honor it, leave space for it, and acknowledge it.

So. What was really here for me in these feelings of being irked by other people's excitement?

Fear.

I was scared shitless.

Fear is a tricky little bugger. For the most part, of most days after treatment, I was doing pretty fantastic. I was feeling better, stronger; I had some sense of normalcy creeping back into my life. I had started high dose IV Vitamin C during the last week of my treatment, and after six weeks of being bedridden, in short order the cloud of depression waned. I had enough energy to walk the dogs, socialize, take on some yard work, and 53 days after being done with treatment I rode in my first mounted shooting competition. We did terribly and had a ton of fun. Things were looking up.

But. For some parts of other days, I would have moments of paralyzing terror. Usually, it would be while doing something that I love, like riding my horse down the road with the birds chirping, the sun rising, those moments of absolute peace when that the sneaky thought came in and said, "What if this is the last two months you have to do this? What if you die?"

This internal commentary would trigger me to lean into fear when people were so excited that I was done treatment. My fear would speak up and remind me I might still die. I mean, we all will die, but like - sooner than I want.

The fear wanted to paralyze me, protect me, keep me "safe" and warm. AKA: stop me living my life. It said, "You better not enjoy life too fiercely. It could all be taken away in an instant. Best to just sit back, not love things so much, so hard. If you settle down with this idea of living in greatness, if your health does go south, the life you're leaving wouldn't have been that great anyway. So take it down a notch. Heaven is probably better than Netflix anyway."

During the peak of these feelings, which occurred in the two months post-treatment, I went to see my acupuncturist/energy healer. It was the first time I had seen him since I finished conventional treatment, and he had assisted me immensely with my side effects of chemo. Before we started the session, we got to catch up about life post-treatment and the proverbial question of "how I'm doing." Suddenly, it all came out there on the couch in his basement like he was my therapist. I told him my truth, about how I was doing well, but how hard it was when the thought crossed my mind: will this be my last ride? My final walk with the dogs? My last dinner with friends? My last sunset? My last drive with the sunroof open?

I continued my story and told him I was doing my very best to change my perspective when fear came knocking and try to combat it with feelings of gratitude for each opportunity, regardless of whether it's the last or I have a thousand left to come.

He smiled at me gently and said, "Isn't that how we all should live?

Whoa, grasshopper.

As he circled his arms around him in universal expansiveness, he continued to say, "Not in a reckless abandon kind of way, but in terms of living your truth, in the present, in the embodiment of gratefulness. This all, any day, could be any one of our last days." He went on to share his experience with near death. He gets it, like gets it gets it, because he's lived through it, too.

When I watch the news (which I do not often do), I hear so frequently of people who don't get a second chance at life like I did. Their life gets taken in an instant in an accident, an attack, an overdose, and they don't get the chance to choose again. To enjoy again. To be grateful again. Even for one more day. When I hear those stories, my heart aches, and then I think to myself, even though I had cancer, I don't have it all that bad. If I have five months, five years, or 50 (#goals), I want to do all I can every day to focus on my second chance at life, not my second chance at death. Hearing those stories makes me focus on being grateful. I have this second chance to choose again.

We need more people to share their stories. It's why I felt compelled to write this book. Experiences are more powerful than anything any of us will learn in a classroom. Look at how we honour scripture with so much more rigour than any textbook. It's full of personal stories and lessons. I am not sharing my tale out of pity; I am sharing this out of a plea. I sit back and watch so many people just living on the outer edge of potential tragedy, and I say in my head every day: "Don't let it come to tragedy before you change. Live. Live every day. You have the power to live your best life without almost dying first."

I struggle to understand why the people closest to me don't hear my story and change. I have more of an influence over strangers than my own family and friends. I watch their snaps, their stories, their posts of their sugar and starch-filled diets, of their kid's consumption of sugar and starch-filled treats. They say, "I wish I could learn how to eat like you." And inside I cry, "YOU CAN! YOU SHOULD!" Because if I can go from the most undomesticated goddess on the planet, eating nothing but chicken fingers and pizzas... you can choose to learn to eat healthy too.

But it's not my place to make them change their lives. I love and accept every one of them as they are, and I pray for them that their life path won't involve critical illness. On the other hand, I will not stop telling my story because I believe society has accepted mediocre health as normal. As standard. I believe we deserve better, to feel better. I will not stop advocating for the healthiest experience we can have on earth. That being said, we also need more people telling stories. Perhaps that's why I'm here, doing my thing, speaking my words, even though I might still die. Part of me didn't want to write my book BECAUSE I might still die. Then I realized that was my feelings of shame creeping back in, that if I write the book and I die, I've failed. Instead, now I look at this as a calling and think if I can get my story out and inspire even one person to radically embrace this human experience and live the hell out of it even more than they already were that will be enough. It will be a start. Because once they are inspired, maybe they will tell their story too. So regardless of when we live or die, through our stories, we can change the world.

25

RHONDA

Throughout all of my treatment, my diagnosis, the entire the experience, I never hated my cancer.

The trends out there - the hashtags, people telling me to kick cancer's ass, to "fight" it, "f*ck cancer," "you messed with the wrong b*tch," - none of that ever resonated with me. If you support someone with cancer, it may be beneficial to ask how they want to treat their recovery.

I didn't want to fight her. Instead, I named her. Rhonda.

I talked to her, I listened to her, I negotiated with her.

I told her that I knew she had once been a good cell, and for whatever reason, turned in to a bad cell. I didn't know her past, and I wasn't going to judge her for it. But I would love her for it. I journaled to her, and I went to energy sessions with her. I made space for her and gave her a choice.

I told her that she could choose to turn good again, or she would die. She was free to choose, but she was not free from the consequence of her choice. I told her my intention was that I would live, and even if I failed at that, we would both die. So she had the opportunity to change her story heroically, or we would both return to the earth.

In the weeks post-radiation, I remember vividly a TV show I was watching where one of the characters had cancer. They described having cancer as suicide from the inside out. I resonated with it. It fell right in line with my belief that dis-ease causes disease. Disease is a slow, slow suicide.

I knew that getting cancer wasn't necessarily my fault, but it was my responsibility. It wasn't something that happened to me; it happened because of me. To cure it, I surely didn't want to feel hate towards my body because that would mean I was fighting myself. My dis-ease of multiple unhealed relational and sexual traumas was the core reason for me getting cervical cancer. My poor diet had been fuel on the fire, and I was going to take responsibility for it.

I accepted the obligation. We allow cancer to ravage our bodies. I do believe that to be true with every piece of my being. Whether it's what we eat, what we don't eat, the exercise we don't do, the spiritual and emotional work we ignore because it's hard, the generational trauma we are naive to, we are a breeding ground for cancer. So to hate what I created… it just didn't seem right.

Louise Hay said in her cancer meditation, "Incurable simply means IN-curable." I saw an Instagram post once that said, "Remission means - Remember Your Mission." We have to go inside ourselves, do the work, and change our lives at a cellular, soul-bearing level. Hell, the change is for the BETTER, so why do so many people not?

It wasn't lost on me when the doctor told me the side effects of radiation would also ravage my other organs. Some would survive, and others would not, due to the depth and strength of penetration from the radiation beams in concentrated areas. My bowels and bladder would likely recover 100%, but my ovaries would be cooked. My skin may begin to burn and peel, but it also would repair.

So my thinking got to be - well, if my body can heal almost all of that damage - why couldn't my cancer? I had to love Rhonda even harder.

After being done treatment, I believed that Rhonda had reformed. That she, too, may have shed pieces of her past, and my lymphatic system washed them away. What was left of her was well-intended, but we both had work to do to heal the trauma that led us here.

They say that it's usually not the first cancer that kills you. I knew I needed to do everything in my power to love this cancer out of me. One thing I did before I started treatment was I wrote my obituary. I refused to write my will, to ask people to take my animals if I died, so I wrote out the end of my life instead.

Adelle Rosalia Stewart

Date of Death: October 27, 2070

Age: 87

Adelle's soul left this earth peacefully in sleep to begin the process of her next earthly journey.

Just the day prior, she had enjoyed the most beautiful of autumn days with a two-mile walk around her farm on which she lived and thrived for over 50 years.

Adelle was predeceased by her life partner; they found love late in life but had a relationship to be revelled. Truly two whole people who came together – they enjoyed a life full of travel, adventure, laughter, and a true understanding of their human experiences on earth.

Unconventionally, as always – they married in front of just a few friends in a place they both loved – near the water and the mountains. The donkeys were there in spirit.

Since the age of 40, Adelle wintered in the southern US. They had a lovely 20-acre parcel where they, the horses, dogs, and donkeys, made this annual trip to and fro, to enjoy the mild weather and southern sunshine.

Adelle rode and competed in mounted shooting for over 30 years. She competed in Canada and the US on many quarter ponies, reviving the breed as a revered sport horse. She rode until she was 82 and then switched to driving miniature donkeys.

She wrote multiple books through the second half of her life and traveled to speak and share her holistic health and healing soul work messages.

Adelle leaves behind many friends, mentees, proteges, family and loved ones. Known her whole life as an "old soul," Adelle was sought for her views and advice by all who knew her. Her uncanny ability to see two sides to every story and to come up with a happy middle was revered by all who shared a cup of tea as they discussed life's blessings.

Since Adelle regularly connected with all those important to her and didn't believe in funerals, there will be no memorial service. "If I didn't talk to you when I was alive – I don't need you to say goodbye!" was her motto.

Adelle's body will return to the earth, planted under an oak tree. Her tree can be visited on her Canadian farm, but she also reminds you that she is near you all the time.

It would be so easy to flip back to automatic.

Wake, dress, do life, eat (candy), sleep, repeat.

Not 24 hours after finishing this chapter, three months after my treatment ended, I received the news that I am cancer free. I will work for the rest of my life to stay that way.

26

JUST LIKE THAT

As soon as I was diagnosed, I changed my life. Just. Like. That. The day I went home from the appointment with my gynecologist, I cleaned out the house. All the instant foods, simple carbs, frozen pizzas, chips, liquor, sugar, like allll the sugar. Icing sugar, raw sugar, coconut sugar, candy, more candy, chocolate, ice cream, and all of it – goodbye.

Six hours after I had been diagnosed, my cupboards were bare. I had a mile-long list of supplements to take like antioxidants, vitamins, minerals, glucose inhibitors, anti-inflammatories, and instantly I knew my life would never, ever be the same.

After being ashamed of my diagnosis, afraid I would fail and die and be judged for it, I went radio silent to the outside world for the entire three months of my treatment. When I finally started telling people about my diagnosis and word on the street got out, I was floored by the number of people who spoke up and shared they also had cancer at one point in their life. My jaw would almost drop to the floor. They don't talk about it. They still eat sugar. Starch. Wine. Glycemic skyrocketing foods – Why? I couldn't bring myself actually to ask, and many times I would think about my own path and question if I might be wrong. Maybe I scared myself too far into this radical lifestyle change?

All the books I read about cancer survival were from people with stage IV terminal cancers. *How to Starve Cancer. Radical Remission. Dying to Live.* I took their advice to heart, even though I was "only" stage 2. I spoke of Jane McLelland's book *How to Starve Cancer* earlier. In her story, she shares how she had initially been diagnosed with cervical cancer at a lower stage, did the "standard" treatment, made some minor adjustments but, for the most part, went back to her pre-cancer life. Her cancer returned as stage IV, death knocking on her door.

I personally couldn't shake her story. As much as I want to eat all the butter tarts, the donuts, the wine, when I think about it, there's a little angel on my shoulder saying, "What if it comes back?" It makes me want to ask other cancer survivors - What if YOURS comes back? For me, I know that in order to live regret free in case I do have a recurrence, I have to live every day doing my best to stay healthy for the long haul. In doing this, I know that if one day I am on my deathbed due to cancer I won't be lying there wishing I had eaten one more butter tart. I would be lying there knowing I did everything I could to preserve my health, to enjoy life to the fullest, having learned that food doesn't have to equal happiness. I can live without sweets and pizza. What I can't live without is feeling so God damn sick, going through cancer treatment ever again, and living a life shorter than 80 years. So I changed.

Cancer shook my existence to the core. I knew I could look at it like a punishment or a blessing, just like I had my marriage. Punishments are way harder to live an enjoyable life with, so I knew I had to change my attitude. I have the OPPORTUNITY to learn how food can fuel my body. I can gain the skills to make healthy food taste delicious. I get the chance to support this vessel I am in, filling it with love and nourishment so it can take me the distance on this earth journey.

It wasn't and is not always easy to choose this way of life. But it's way easier than being stuck in bed and unable to enjoy life at all. I'm not perfect every single day with my diet, but I'm aware. I am aware that the average fast-food cookie has 18 grams of added sugar in it. I am aware that a pumpkin spice latte has 38 grams of sugar in it. Where I used to have no problem downing three cookies or a box of 10 honey glazed donut holes by myself regularly, now I might have one cookie once every few weeks. Or three donut holes instead of an entire box. I drink carbonated water as a treat instead of alcohol or sugary drinks.

So how much sugar is too much sugar? According to health statistics, the average woman should have no more than 26 grams of added sugar per day - BUT – we eat about 76 grams a day. As a cancer thriver, I'm no average woman anymore, so I don't even consume more than 26 grams of added sugar a week.

If you read this and say to yourself – no way, I can't do that - I don't blame you. We are addicted to sugar. Addicted. But just like drugs and alcohol, sugar does NOTHING of benefit to our bodies. Cancer thrives off sugar. This is a highly debated topic, but one I believe in. The #1 cancer diagnostic tool is the pet scan - that pumps you full of glucose, which cancer cells readily take up and can be seen on the imaging. High dose intravenous vitamin C, same thing. It appears to cancer as glucose, but once the cancer cell takes it up, it oxidizes, creating an environment cancer can't live in, and the vitamin C blows it up. There are insulin-penetrating chemotherapy treatments in other parts of the world that also use glucose to improve the drug's efficiency.

We know this, right? We know this. So, why don't we change? Why don't we hear of someone's cancer diagnosis and say, OMG, she is too young. She's too healthy! If she can get cancer, I can get cancer. Maybe I should take a cold hard look at my life and make some pivots.

But we don't. I didn't either. I had heard of lots of people getting cancer before I did. Mostly older, but some younger people. "Ohhhhh, poor her," "She's so young!" "Fuck Cancer." And we go on with our day. I went on with my day. I took my vitamins, and I ate my lie of a balanced diet. I raised my heart rate a few times a week, usually by running after a stray donkey if I left the gate open.

We are becoming complacent to cancer. To chronic illness. We are numb to it, immune to thinking we could experience it ourselves, then simply accepting it once it arrives. Truthfully, we should shaking in our boots. The odds of a woman getting cancer in her life is one in two. ONE. IN. TWO. So there's me, and there's you. I've had it, so I surely hope it won't be you too. But do you know another woman? Daughter? Mother? Sister? Best friend? Two of the four of those people are at a statistically high risk of the disease. It's too high. It's too high!

Hollywood kills off people with cancer on the regular. I used to not think a thing about it. Now I almost have to turn the TV off when they diagnose someone with it. It has become too regular. We have accepted cancer.

Do you accept cancer? Because that's how we are acting. I say it with such passion because I accepted it too. I thought that "it couldn't happen to me," but then, it did.

When we know better, we can do better, so why aren't we?

My own family hasn't changed. Their daughter could have died from cancer. Their daughter may still die of cancer. I'm only eight months past my diagnosis, so really anything could happen. Why are we so numb to this?

I changed radically, and I know that's not easy for people. If you remember from earlier reading, I'm a significant change kind of gal. Don't move that trinket, but let's cut out sugar overnight. Especially if you are not sick, you don't have to change like me; transformation can be gradual. Do you ever wonder how much better you could feel? Maybe you wish you could sleep through the night or not have that ache in your back or that knock in your knee. What about those headaches? Or how about that weight? I would wager that we can't have a conversation with another human being who doesn't have some sort of chronic peril ailing them.

We are failing our bodies, and they are the only place we have to live.

Please do it. Make a change, I implore you. I know I can't make anyone change, but I damn sure can be an influence for those who are ready to take the challenge. Do it for your kids. Do it for your spouse. Do it for your parents. Do it for you.

Start small. Eat one extra veggie a day until it's easy. Do 10 minutes of exercise a day until it's easy. You'll suddenly find yourself craving that thing you've changed, and you'll want more. Honestly, that's how it works. Don't even cut anything out yet! Just add. Add one thing, make it easy, then add another. Cutting things out like sugar will begin to take care of themselves. You'll then start to take half a teaspoon of sugar less in your coffee. Maybe you'll bake the next dozen cookies with sugar replacement. If you graduate in to change before you are faced with the diagnosis of a life-threatening illness, I hope to God we can start to avoid them altogether.

Because let me say this, if it can be me, it can be you too. And I don't want it to be.

27

UNBURIED

Extreme independence is a trauma response.

Excuse me?

Extreme independence - is a trauma response.

It was a post on Instagram that stopped me in my scrolling tracks.

"That's me," I whispered to myself. It was akin to the feeling I had when I was 8 years old in the reading nook of my classroom. That's me.

I read it while I was writing this book and my entire life suddenly all made sense. I pulled away from the relationship with my mom after my childhood trauma. I didn't feel safe as a young girl and needed to protect myself from others so that I wouldn't feel pain. Losing my first love – any guard I had let down in the arms of his safety went right back up after Graham died. Now twice bitten, the trauma led me to choose toxic relationships that I never had to let my walls down to be in them, some odd false sense of security. Then, when I had met Jack, who I could have actually leaned into, I was so far gone. The pendulum swung too far that an offer of him topping up the windshield fluid in my truck pissed me off. *He's not for me. He is crushing my independence. I can do it myself.* It was the trauma talking. My inner child who had to grow up too fast and then shielded herself from any close relationship in order to protect herself.

Through my life experiences, I had become conditioned to not trust anyone. If I trusted no one, no one could let me down. It felt safe. I felt empowered. I know I needed to feel that way for a time, but after getting cancer, I see a part of my lesson: learning how to trust again.

As I am working through it, I am extremely sensitive to anyone's actions towards me. Not calling when they said they would, failing on a commitment, cancelling a lunch – they hurt me deeply, like salt in a wound, except this time I will push through. These instances make me want to crawl back to the safety of my inner world of independence and introverted-ness. I know I can rely on me; it is uncomfortable being out there asking for help, for company, for favors, especially when you're let down.

There was a foreshadowing of this lesson as I went through treatment. I was fortunate to have a few friends who innately understood this. Most everyone said, "If you need anything, let me know." To which my inner child spoke up and said, "We don't need anyone, thank you."

So some of these special friends, knew what I needed, and just did it. One pal kept a countdown to my end of treatment. She would text me every day – every day – and sometimes, just as the evening would come to a close when I hadn't heard from her yet and wanted to take it as ammunition that no one can really be there for me, in would come her text tone "Happy twelve days left!" She never missed one. My best friend would scour Pinterest and send me recipes until I said yes to one that I would eat. The next day she would drop off soups and freezer meals at my door. Another organized a yard cleanup day to get all my spring work done on the ranch.

The biggest thing that stands out to me about this is that none of them ever asked. I didn't have to tell them what I needed or wanted. I didn't have the capacity, not only from being sick but because I had never relied on anyone for as long as I can remember. They told me, "I am making you soup; let me know which recipe you prefer." "I am organizing a spring-cleaning day at your place. Can you get a list together, and we'll be there Tuesday."

When I didn't know what I needed or how to ask for it, they did. It felt both good and terrifying to trust another human being for the first time in a long time.

I let my mom be my mom. She would come over, tell me what to eat, to brush my hair, to go sit outside for a few minutes. Some days I would resist, and other days I leaned in. I didn't even realize at the time that I was letting little Adelle experience having a mom for the first time in a long time. What was even more revolutionary, was as long as I didn't push her away, she kept coming back.

I am still not in a place where I am welcoming love into my life. Some people search so hard and do all their energy work to manifest their soulmate. Then there's me, and I look at my king-sized bed where I starfish each night on one side, and my two dogs stretch out on the other. "There's no room for anyone else," I tell myself. As it stands right now – I can't see the forest for the trees on this one yet. I can't imagine letting anyone get that close to me, into my house, my bed, my heart.

As I continue my healing journey, I see this and know I have much work to do. Some days I feel as if I am not doing the work fast enough. I will visit my energy healer who connects with my guides, and I am nervous that I'm not fixing it all fast enough, fast enough to beat the cancer coming back. "I still don't want a life partner, or anyone," I tell her. "It's not normal, and I know that, but I just can't even bring myself to write a goal or intention to welcome it – I simply don't want it."

"You're doing just fine," they always say. Awareness is the first step to healing, my guides assure me. And although it frustrates the hell out of me that I do not yet have an answer or a direct path to follow in fully healing my past trauma, I am trusting, surrendering, that I am on my way.

I am aware of the delicate balance that lies before me. Some days there are things that paralyze me from doing what I dream of. I want to spend winters in the south – and I already work from home, which means I could work from anywhere. But there's a voice inside of me that says, "You can't do that alone – you can't travel 5,000 miles with a trailer full of animals and put up shop somewhere you've never spent more than a week in." I let that voice keep me in Canada. I also have tendencies to want to toss all responsibility onto someone else and rely on them to do hard things for me. "That fence board isn't an essential fence board." And I'll wait until my dear friend Gus passes through town for work because he always gives me a hand when he does.

There's a balance as I heal… where my goal is to have a healthy buffer of independence to get things done myself when I need to and ask for help when things are really hard.

We all have work to do on trauma; I guarantee you that. When I was going through treatment, I listened every night to Louise Hay's Cancer meditation. She said we are all "victims of victims" and then victims of our own unhealed human experience. In my opinion, this is why the world seems to be getting worse, not better. We are not unpacking our bags full of baggage and then they are unintentionally passed down to our children, who will have their own burdens to bear already. If I had stayed in my relationship with Mark and had a child, we would have raised it just as damaged as we both were. My grandfather was an alcoholic, so by taking control of my relationship with alcohol, I am breaking that cycle, too. We all have some form of trauma, and the world will begin to become a better place when we dare to unbury it for good.

The first step to healing is simply understanding that. On what comes next, I can offer no good advice because I haven't traveled up that mountain and come down the other side yet. Maybe in my next book. My current intention is that "I am open to receiving love and quality relationships into my life." I don't know how I'm going to get there, or when I will, but by believing in the universe, the divine, god, I understand I don't have to know those things as long as I stay committed to receiving, and release control of the outcome.

In the meantime, I have a lot of other things to work on anyway. I need to learn how to be let my walls down without retreating to the safety of my fierce independence. If pain can't get in, neither can love. I know that much now.

We must take responsibility for healing individually. Sometimes the wounds are old, sometimes they are fresh, and sometimes they aren't even directly ours but the result of decades of generational trauma. What happened to me as a child was not my fault, but it is my responsibility to heal. And that healing, plus taking care of what I feed my body, is how I know that I will prevent my cancer from ever returning.

28

THE SUNDAY FRIEND

Somewhere along the line, things changed with a lot of people, with most people. Many of my relationships grew closer, and people I had considered acquaintances were now dear friends.

Other friendships grew apart. About six months after my treatment ended, I noticed that I was no longer the "call for a good time" pal, for the Friday night escapades, the shenanigans, the music, the dancing.

I was now the Sunday friend. The coffee at 10 in the morning friend.

Do people make these decisions intentionally? Say, "let's not call her because she doesn't drink." I don't believe they do. I don't feel they do because I also don't believe Mark intentionally thought to himself each day, "I want to control her, make her my puppet." I think these actions themselves are examples of trauma responses and generational baggage, that these actions occur due to some subconscious exclusion with no perception of how things used to be compared to how they were being presented now.

But still, even if it wasn't conscious, the shift hurt. I felt pitied. They were protecting me from something that I wasn't choosing to be shielded from—not inviting me so I wouldn't have to watch them drink.

I quit drinking the day I found out I had cancer. Along with sugar and shitty food I ate, I had found myself drinking daily for the last year or so. It had become my reward for making it through the day. I had a regimented schedule that surrounded sitting down at the end of the day, work done, horses rode, responsibilities acquitted, to take a deep breath and sit in the sway-backed Adirondack chair, look out on to my beautiful backyard, and crack a cold one.

It was only ever just one. One was all I needed to enjoy a soft buzz while I waited for my pizza to bake, and by the time dinner was over, I was stone-cold sober. It was the perfect relationship with alcohol, and looking back, a really negative coping strategy. I'd never been a heavy drinker at any point in my life – I can't handle being hungover. But this one drink per day was a happy medium between taking the edge off and not getting a hangover. Clearly, those parameters didn't make me an alcoholic... right?

Plus, it was harder for me to cut out sugar than it was for me to cut out alcohol, so that was on the side of my argument that I wasn't an alcoholic as well, right?

I'm a way more prominent advocate for pushing clean eating and being sugar-free than I am against drinking, which counts against me being an alcoholic, too, right?

Sugar and alcohol had been my negative coping strategies, the things that pacified me from facing what I really needed to in my life. Initially, I argued with myself that they didn't soothe me from my loneliness because I wasn't lonely. Except maybe I was. The soft buzz from the wine, or the addictive high from the sugar, temporarily filled a void in me that was blocking another human from providing me with those feelings through talk, touch, and affection.

I have sat and wondered why... why do I love and want that sugar rush so much? For seven months, I have been trialling and mostly erroring with healthy sugar-free baking snacks. I have not been able to get over the craving for sweets. I am only trying to replace it with something sweet that isn't sugar. I couldn't figure out why I needed that comfort. It didn't make sense to me. On one hand, I have realized and acknowledged that I had built a fortress around myself, protecting me from letting anyone in. And on the other hand, I realized I had a sugar and alcohol addiction, but I didn't understand how they related to each other.

They were providing me with the feelings I lacked from human connection.

This is my work to do.

The path forward isn't clear. All I know is that it will be up. I have been struggling with my diet and making fear-based decisions not to eat sugar or drink alcohol. Excess sugar causes inflammation, my liver processes alcohol, and I don't want to tax my organs with detoxing my body from booze and glucose when it has other essential jobs to do. I would look at others and can't believe the things they choose to eat. Inside of that behaviour, I see now I was projecting. "You just finished a 75-day workout challenge, and on day 76, you've cracked the bottle?" Wow. "You just watched me go through cancer, and you're eating ramen noodles for supper." I can't believe it. "Sugar feeds cancer, and you're letting your kid eat a brownie?" What's the matter with you.

I see now that it was all the matter - with me. Judgement of others is the first instance we need to look inwards. I know this. I've read the books. Gabby Bernstine's book *Judgement Detox* was one of the most challenging books I've ever tried to read. It makes you so…. accountable. I wasn't ready to read it many times, and I don't actually think I've ever finished it. Time to go back to it now, I guess.

I've contemplated my position on my diet. *Should I have "cheat days?" Can I eat sugar like everyone else?* What if I get cancer again, and if I did incorporate those things back in my life, could I live with myself if that happens?

Then I look on those thoughts and say to myself, there I go now, living out of fear. Living looking over my shoulder at the shadow of cancer is as toxic as the sugar I'd consume.

I have come to a balance and realized I don't need to be a martyr and take a hard and fast approach to sugar and my diet. Yes, I do think I have to eat clean 95% of the time, but I now also see that the coping strategy sugar and alcohol were for me, are for me, and is indicative of more inward work I have yet to do. This work is in relation to my trauma response, directly tied to my discomfort of letting people into my life.

I see the path more clearly now. That once I climb this mountain, do the deep work that will allow me to let my guard down, to stop seeing the negative about sharing my life with someone, and be at a place of welcoming, when the time is right for that person to enter my life, once that work is done, I know now that I will be able to indulge in a sweet treat or enjoy a soft buzz and it absolutely won't contribute to my cancer coming back.

Thank you for reading this chapter, for watching how I changed my life before your eyes, for bearing witness to how I find my next climb. This is my secret to the summits. I do this deep, dark hard work by writing, bearing down, bleeding out my heart and soul on to paper. I am two different people when I write. I am my spirit and my human experience, soul and brain, coming together to work in harmony on this earth. Writing allows me to be both of these beings at once; as I get the facts out on paper, it clears the path for divine intervention to flow through me and allows me to see clearly how I can become the next best version of myself.

I hope you're enjoying this journey.

29

BETWEEN THE PEAKS

It took my experience with cancer to understand the meaning of life. It took frequent, relentless ups and downs that rolled in like waves from the ocean to get it. Life is not about conquering one mountain, one summit, one peak. Maybe that's why mountain climbers get addicted to the summit and can't stop going up the next mountain. Because this is what life is, all of it. A constant summit to the top and descent to the valley, over and over and over again. The secret to realizing this, should we choose to accept each journey, is knowing that we get better at climbing. We grow stronger, have more tools, develop better insight, and use supports to get there safely - even if the next mountain is more dangerous than the last.

When we keep saying yes, the difficulty and intensity of the climb will keep increasing. We may stay at the top of a mountain for a long time, but descent is inevitable. That is where I falsely assumed safety and stability were - at the top. But exploring this now, I know that in real life mountaineering, the summit is the most dangerous place to be, and climbers don't stay there very long. The weather can change in an instant, and without proper calculation and the strong check of the ego, it can mean the difference between life and death. Through the process of writing this book and figuring this out, I believe, is quite simply why "bad things happen to good people." Good people are the enlightened, the hard workers, the constant improvers. But when we stay at the top too long, life reminds us that it's a nice place to visit, but we aren't meant to live there.

I got comfortable and stayed at the top of my last mountain for too long. Then I fell, swiftly and far, nowhere but down. Lucky for me, I survived. I get another chance to climb again, hopefully, many more times. I understand this now and accept my responsibility for this disease, my trauma, and its healing. It is so much more than cancer. It's healing my inner child, the one who doesn't remember love and affection or the feeling of safety. It's forgiving my childhood abuser, my ex-husband, and myself for leaving Jack.

Since I never had children and now can't, I will give myself to our younger generation in any way I can, and hopefully to the masses. Parent by parent is a long and winding road to salvation, so although we need good parents committed to ending their generational trauma one child at a time, for those who are not ready to do that, we need teachers and storytellers like me to help them find their way when they may be prepared to leave the false safety of the summit they are on and descend to their next valley.

I don't know what the future holds, except there will be more mountains. I also no longer believe the summit is the goal, but rather the destination is the next valley. Valleys provide shade, shelter, flora and fauna, all the things we need to survive and thrive. The valleys are the safe havens of our lives. The mountains are our lesson, harsh, unsustainable, barren and dangerous. The valley is our reward for learning from that journey. My next peak might be more cancer if I don't understand and heal my trauma properly. But if it is not cancer, I know at least that it will be something else. This time though, I expect it will be coming, and I accept and welcome the challenge. Maybe it will be love, or perhaps it will be disaster. We don't know where our next mountain lesson will appear; we can only decide whether we accept the climb.

I will always say yes.

ABOUT THE AUTHOR

Adelle Stewart is a Writer, Speaker, Executive Director, and Boss Babe. Adelle owns and runs a company called Prime Equine, offering boutique horse boarding, equine nutrition and health courses, and a myriad of retail products for cowgirls and their horses.

Adelle is a Certified Life Coach, putting her skills to work every day through her social media channels and her blog, encouraging everyone around her to live their best life.

She advocates for holistic healthcare, natural products, and sugar free, clean eating diets. Through her own trial and error, she now represents some of the best products on the market which she shares with others.

You can find Adelle's writings, recipes and daily musings at:

- @adellerosalia on Facebook, Instagram, Pinterest and Twitter

Clean eating recipes and thought essays at:

- www.adellerosalia.com

Natural health support products at:

- www.globallee.com/adellestewart

- www.seacretdirect.com/adellestewart

All things horses at:

- www.primeequine.ca

For media and speaking inquiries:

- adellerosalia@gmail.com

ACKNOWLEDGMENTS

Writing this book was both the easiest and most difficult thing I have ever done in my life. My memoir would have never got finished without the love and support of my dear friends cheering me on, asking about the progress, and sharing in their excitement in buying a book written by their friend.

Through sharing the journey as I wrote, I reconnected with people from my past, both old friends and extended family. We made meaningful connections during a time of disconnect through the global pandemic of Covid-19, and for that, I am grateful.

Thank you to my parents and my brother for not prying for details as I wrote. This story was hard to tell and having to make considerations for how everyone would feel about how they appeared in this book weighed heavily on me; my family's portrayal meant the most to me. I was able to write my truth, recognize many revelations, and heal generational trauma by getting my story out on paper. My family has always been my biggest cheerleaders, even though I didn't always know how to accept their support.

Kelsy, Alyssa, Karel, Jay, Naomi, Bart, Julia, Twila, Edie, Brenda, Leanne, and Jackie, I consider you my personal cheerleaders throughout my treatment. Each of you contributed to my recovery in one way or another and held my secret close as the only people outside my family who knew what was going on during that dark, difficult, enlightening time of my life. I had been so afraid to lean on people, but you all showed me that I could.

To my writing mentor and coach Jennifer Sparks from Stoke Publishing – Thank you. The opportunity to win your Author Launch Pad scholarship is a major reason this book is on paper. I had no idea where to start before I met you. Your self publishing program, marketing advice, and overall support is 100% the difference between this book coming to life versus remaining in my head as a wish.

I would like to thank my oncologists, for their expertise and support and willingness to put up with my thousands of questions and their openness to listening to my advocacy of incorporating alternative treatment into my recovery. To my naturopaths, physiotherapists, energy healers, massage therapist, counsellor, acupuncturist, and integrative physician, I truly don't believe I would be healed without you all on my team, thank you.

To every person who has been a part of my life - good or bad – thank you. You were either a part of my life as a blessing, or a lesson, and I am grateful for either, as I am the woman I am today because of our experience together.

To my readers, thank you for coming along on this journey of mine.

I will see you all on the next climb.

Made in the USA
Middletown, DE
18 February 2021